Love Freaks

Iain Heggie

(Based on *Double Inconstancy* by Marivaux)

Methuen

Methuen

1 3 5 7 9 10 8 6 4 2

Published in Great Britain in 2002 by
Methuen Publishing Limited,
215 Vauxhall Bridge Road,
London SW1V 1EJ

Copyright © 2002 Iain Heggie

The author has asserted his moral rights

Methuen Publishing Limited Reg. No. 3543167

A CIP catalogue record is available from the British Library

ISBN 0 413 77258 6

Typeset by SX Composing DTP, Rayleigh, Essex
Printed and bound in Great Britain by
Cox & Wyman Ltd, Reading, Berkshire

FIRST PERFORMED AT THE TRON THEATRE, GLASGOW ON 16 MAY 2002.

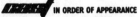 **IN ORDER OF APPEARANCE**

Damon Sludden / Ronan O'Donnell	Brian Ferguson
Marlon O'Donnell / Ringo Sludden	Callum Cuthbertson
Whitney Colqhoun	Gabriel Quigley
Britney Colqhoun	Carmen Peraccini
Celine McAnespie	Julie Austin
Jarvis Hood	Paul Riley

production

Director	Graham Eatough
Designer	Evelyn Barbour
Lighting Designer	Dave Shea
Sound Designer	John Scott
Wardrobe Supervisor	Anna Lau
Production Manager	Jo Masson
Stage Manager	Craig Fleming
Deputy Stage Manager	Kirsty Paton
Assistant Stage Manager	Sian Mitchell MacGregor
Set Construction	J&B Scenery

The Company would particularly like to thank:
Rod Hall, The RSAMD, Dundee Rep, Grae Cleugh, Clare Yuille,
Alan Tripney, Sam Heughan, Mark Melville, Alana Hood,
Kieran Brown, Peter Robertson, Toni Frutin, Frances Thorburn,
Beverly Rye, Brian Ferguson, John-Jo Thacker, Lindsay Gillan,
Atalanta Advertising & Design and K&M Photography.

the company

JULIE AUSTIN // Celine McAnespie

Julie's first appearance on stage was in a Tron Theatre production of Ghost Story in 1985 - when she was only wee! So she's dead pleased to be back now that she's a proper grownup! Since graduating from RSAMD she has been busy working as an actor that so far hasn't been found out. Her theatre work includes: Brave (Communicado/ SOP); Beauty and the Beast, Cinderella, Romeo & Juliet, The Hypochondriac (Royal Lyceum); A Midsummer Night's Dream (Arches); Damaged Goods (Roughcast); Cinderella, Bold Girls (Cumbernauld). Her film and television work includes The Magdalene Sisters, Women Talking Dirty, Complicity, Braveheart and Crow Road. Julie has also worked extensively for BBC Radio 4, most recently as Mairi in the trilogy, Faith, Hope & Charity.

EVELYN BARBOUR // Designer

Evelyn trained at Glasgow School of Art and her theatre work includes: Cave Dwellers, 24 Hours, Caledonia Dreaming, Valley Song, Act Your Age, It's Not Enough (7:84 Theatre Company, Scotland); Dr Korczak's Example, King Matt (TAG); Moving Objects, Aladdin, Romeo and Juliet, The Price (Brunton Theatre Company); The Laird's New Kilt, Labyrinth, The Loch Ness Affair (Wee Stories); The Princess and the Goblin (Dundee Rep); Learning the Paso Doble (Stellar Quines); Working Legs (Birds of Paradise); Showtime (Scottish Opera for All); Tongues (7:84/ Birds of Paradise); Albertine in Five Times (Clyde Unity); Lazybed (Traverse Theatre Company); Dave's Last Laugh (Tron Theatre Company); Airport (Suspect Culture); Sooans'Nicht (Castlemilk People's Theatre); Dracula, The Winter's Tale, Women Beware Women, Tis Pity She's a Whore, All's Well That Ends Well, The Importance of Being Earnest, Measure for Measure, Much Ado About Nothing, Albert Herring, The Hypochondriac, The Europeans, The Crucible, The House of Bernarda Alba (RSAMD); Giant Steps (Visible Fictions); Waiting for Godot (Tongue Tied Theatre Company).

CALLUM CUTHBERTSON // Marlon O'Donnell / Ringo Sludden

Callum has worked extensively in Scottish theatre. His recent work includes: The News at When...2001 (7:84 Theatre Company, Scotland); Lament (Suspect Culture); a rehearsed reading of San Diego at the Tron Theatre. Other recent work includes, Lazybed, Passing Places and First Bites (The Traverse); A Little Rain, 24 Hours, Outside Broadcast and News At When (7:84 Theatre Company, Scotland); Mainstream (Suspect Culture); King Matt (TAG Theatre Co). His film and TV work includes Rab C Nesbitt, Take the High Road, Ruffian Hearts, and Breaking the Waves. He has also written two award winning short films: How High the Castle Walls and Goodbye Happy Ending.

GRAHAM EATOUGH // Director

After studying Drama and English Literature at Bristol University, Graham co-founded Suspect Culture Theatre Company with writer David Greig in 1990. As well as conceiving, directing and performing in eleven shows for Suspect Culture, he has been the Company's Artistic Director since 1995 when the Company based itself in Glasgow. During this time he has focused the Company's work on the development of a distinctive performance style that relies on abstracted stage pictures, gesture, and the integration of text, music and choreographed movement. Recent productions for Suspect Culture include Lament, Casanova, Candide 2000, Mainstream, Timeless and Airport.

Graham has also worked extensively as a director in Milan with C.R.T. theatre company and Madrid where he directed an outdoor workshop production of Purcell's The Fairy Queen in 1998. Theatre work outwith Suspect Culture includes directing and choreographing a new chamber opera for the Beckett Festival in Glasgow in 2000, Something There and devising and directing 7:84's Election '99 and Outside Broadcast. Film work includes performances in Hold Back the Night (Parallax Films), Goodbye Happy Ending (Falling Water Films) and The Stalker's Apprentice (STV Films).

BRIAN FERGUSON // Damon Sludden / Ronan O'Donnell

Brian graduated from the RSAMD last summer. Last seen in She Stoops to Conquer (Perth Rep), Brian's other theatre appearances include Observe the Sons of Ulster Marching Towards the Somme (Citizens) and Timelapse (The Arches). Television appearances include the new BBC Drama Series Rock Face and the Newfoundland Short, Last Legs.

IAIN HEGGIE // Writer

Iain is one of Scotland's leading playwrights and also teaches acting & improvisation at the Royal Scottish Academy of Music and Drama. For the past two years he has won Scotsman Fringe Firsts for his plays King of Scotland (2000) and Wiping My Mother's Arse (2001). Past work includes: A Wholly Healthy Glasgow, American Bagpipes, An Experienced Woman Gives Advice, The Sex Comedies, Lust and Politics In The Park.

Iain made his directorial debut in April 2001 with the Scottish Premiere of Martin McDonagh's The Beauty Queen of Lenanne at the Tron Theatre. He is currently directing a production of Don Juan for the RSAMD.

CARMEN PIERACCINI // Britney Colqhoun

Since graduating from the RSAMD, Carmen has had a successful career in theatre, film and television. Carmen's theatre performances have included Losing Alec and Like a Virgin in which she played the lead part of Maxine (Cumbernauld Theatre Scottish and Irish tours 2000 & 2001). Film and TV appearances include Late Night Shopping (Ideal World / Film Four), Taggart (STV), Brotherly Love (BBC), Glasgow Kiss (BBC), My Life So Far and the award winning Small Faces (dir. Gillies MacKinnon). She also played the co-lead part of Nina in 3 successful series of the BBC Children's show GFORCE.

GABRIEL QUIGLEY // Whitney Colqhoun

A graduate from the University of Glasgow, Gabriel has had an extensive career on both screen and stage. Recent theatre productions include Burning Bright (V.amp Productions, The Tramway), Top Girls (The New Vic, Stoke on Trent), Mainstream (Suspect Culture), Outside Now (Prada), Dissent (7:84), Chic Nerds (Traverse Theatre Company) and Trainspotting (Citizens Theatre). Television appearances include Chewin' The Fat (Comedy Unit/BBC), Only an Excuse (Comedy Unit/BBC), Glasgow Kiss (BBC), Taggart (STV), Haywire (BBC), Life Support (BBC) and Bumping The Odds (BBC).

PAUL RILEY // Jarvis Hood

Paul's first job upon leaving school was at a greyhound stadium, but like the Hare, he always wanted to know what was round the bend. A three year stretch at RSAMD followed and since 1991 Paul has worked extensively in both television and theatre. Theatre credits include: Trainspotting (F & G Productions); Under Milk Wood (Brunton); Purple Dust, Glengarry Glenross and Midsummer Night's Dream (Arches). Television credits include Taggart, High Road, Rab C Nesbitt and most recently writing and appearing in Chewin the Fat. He is currently filming a new sit com, Still Game, which features the 'Old Men' from Chewin the Fat.

DAVE SHEA // Lighting Designer

Design work includes: Cave Dwellers, A Little Rain, Goldie and the Bears (7:84 Theatre Company, Scotland); The Golden Ass (Suspect Culture); Our Bad Magnet (Tron/ Borderline); Master of the House (Stride); Someone Who'll Watch Over Me (Company Theatre); Waiting Room (Complete); Ashes to Ashes (Ghostown); Scott of the Antartic (Big Like Texas); Marat Sade (RSAMD).
Dave is currently Production Manager for 7:84 Theatre Company, Scotland and was Deputy Technical Manager at the Tron Theatre from 1995 - 1997.

Tron Theatre, Glasgow
an artistic history

The Tron Theatre was established as a theatre club in 1979 (going fully public in 1989), rising from the ashes of the destroyed Close Theatre, based at the Citizens Theatre, Glasgow.

Originally based in the Victorian Bar of the Tron whilst the Kirk itself was transformed into the auditorium, the Tron has become a leading player in Scottish theatre.

Under the Artistic leadership of Michael Boyd (1986 to 1996) - now Associate Director of the Royal Shakespeare Company - the Tron established itself as a powerhouse of both new writing and dynamic productions of classic texts, making full use of available Scottish talent. Leading artists to emerge from this period include Alan Cumming, Forbes Masson, Peter Mullan, Craig Ferguson and Siobhan Redmond, as well as musician Craig Armstrong (Baz Luhrmann's Romeo and Juliet & Moulin Rouge). Many of these artists still continue an association with the Tron.

Among the highlights of Michael Boyd's tenure at the Tron were a landmark production of Macbeth (starring Iain Glen), an award winning adaptation of Janice Galloway's The Trick is to Keep Breathing (Glasgow, London, Toronto), the introduction of Quebec playwright Michel Tremblay to Scotland (The Guid Sisters), and a string of popular and unique Glaswegian Christmas shows.

From 1996 to 1999 the company was led by Irina Brown and productions included David Greig's award winning The Cosmonaut's Last Message to the Woman He Once Loved in the Former Soviet Union, as well as a dynamic international programme. The works of Russian and Italian playwrights, Alexei Shipenko and Vittorio Francesci, respectively, were given their British premieres at the Tron in Irina's tenure. Further than the Furthest Thing was commissioned and developed by Irina Brown whilst Artistic Director of the Tron. The show was co-produced with the Royal National Theatre and played the Edinburgh Festival and the Royal National Theatre in 2000 before touring South Africa in 2001.

The Tron is currently being run as a producer-led theatre with an exciting combination of home productions and visiting work. The Tron Theatre Company's recent productions have included the World premiere of Scottish writer Douglas Maxwell's play Our Bad Magnet, the multi-award winning production of Further than the Furthest Thing by Zinnie Harris and the Scottish Premiere of Martin McDonagh's The Beauty Queen of Leenane, directed by Iain Heggie. Future plans include a major season of Canadian theatre in October 2002 (in collaboration with Six Stages Festival, Toronto) and a new commissioned Christmas show by Forbes Masson.

The Tron is also an established receiving theatre on the small/middle scale as well as a major venue for many of Glasgow's festivals including Big Big Country, Si Cuba!, Celtic Connections, Glasgow International Jazz Festival, New Territories and Glasgay!

The combination of historic, listed buildings, stunning new architecture, popular bars and restaurant and most importantly, vital artistic programme continues to make the Tron one of Scotland's and indeed Britain's, leading theatre venues.

Iron Theatre staff

Introduction

I was first introduced to Marivaux by Mike Alfreds's great productions in the early eighties. It was one of the experiences that led me into trying to write for theatre. So when the opportunity came up to do a modern adaptation, I couldn't easily say no. Molière, the writer of broad and racy social satires, is extremely popular in Scotland. Whether Marivaux could be popular in Scotland remains to be seen. His plays are like social experiments which put psychological processes under the microscope. The question he persistently asks is: can love be manipulated? The nearest contemporary equivalent might be TV experiments like *Big Brother*, which seem to strike a chord in us all. Marivaux might come over to us as overly diabolical, triumphalist or refined. But many very successful contemporary plays and films are exactly those things. In a famous role-reversal experiment, Michael Billington directed a Marivaux play which was reviewed by Terry Hands, then artistic director of the RSC. I never saw the production, but Mr Hands criticised it on the grounds that the characters were not sufficiently monstrous. Now, I know I didn't see the production and I know nothing about Mr Hands's experience of life, but frankly the idea that Marivaux's characters are monsters seems to me nothing less than monstrous! To me, they are all too human. At once triumphalist and vulnerable, self-deluded and self-aware, knowing and gullible, competitive and compassionate, inconsistent and yet all too predictable. Maybe it's just that RSC actors are especially saintly and spending half his life in rehearsal with them had lent Mr Hands a rose-tinted view of reality!

Though the central part of the plot and Marivaux's main concerns are still very much in evidence, the process of adaptation has taken my version of *Double Inconstancy* so far from the original that the question of why Marivaux is not produced in Scotland will arguably remain untested by this production. I am no believer in faithful adaptations. I changed the title to *Love Freaks* because I think *Double*

Inconstancy – at least in English – must go down as one of the worst titles ever written. (Mentioning it to a friend on the phone recently made her giggle. While I was glad to have confirmation that it is a bad title, I didn't think it was particularly funny. It turned out that the listener thought I had said *Double Incontinence*. Which, as they say, says it all.) I wanted to shift the focus away from marriage, which is not the high-stakes issue it once was, to one of commitment, which seems to be one of the huge imponderables of our time. The advantage of Marivaux's characters to a certain extent living a privileged existence means that love processes can be focused on more purely. But nevertheless I wanted to bring the play closer to the world I know. The one where people have to sort their love issues out at the same time as find enough money to live on and work out what to believe in!

Iain Heggie

For Vivien and for Stewart

Love Freaks

Characters

Marlon O'Donnell, *the owner of Costly Coffee, an international chain of coffee shops.*
Damon Sludden, *the son of Ringo.*
Ringo Sludden, *employee of O'Donnell.*
Whitney Colqhoun, *training manager and Marlon's lover.*
Ronan O'Donnell, *son of Marlon and heir to the Costly Coffee chain.*
Britney Colqhoun, *Whitney's younger sister.*
Celine McAnespie, *assistant manager at Costly Coffee.*
Jarvis Hood, *ecowarrior and assistant manager at Best Burgers*

Setting

The Ayrshire training centre for Costly Coffee in the grounds of Monknock Castle and estate, the fortified home of the self-made multimillionaire and owner of Costly Coffee, Marlon O'Donnell.

Acknowledgement

Thanks to the students of the RSAMD and the Tron Theatre for their help with script development.

Act One

The Costly Coffee training centre. A mock-up of a coffee house. On two levels. The upper mezzanine floor is divided roughly on a diagonal; there is a walled office to one side, with a window to the front, through which we can see desks, chairs, phones, computers, a map of the world indicating the varying density of Costly Coffee shops across the globe with big target arrows focused on America and a door opening on to the open side of the mezzanine. On the open side, which is part of the coffee-house mock-up, are some tables and chairs, possibly a door at the back of the mezzanine which could lead to toilets and stairs down to the ground level. On the ground level are tables, chairs, couches maybe, less densely concentrated than would be the case in an actual coffee house, a serving/kitchen area, food, coffee equipment, a till, dishwasher, sink and draining board, etc. with a faked public entrance and a private entrance. In the middle of the stage is a suitcase and bag, labelled and ready to travel with. There should be considerable mess on the tables and floor as a result of a staff party or leaving do the night before. There might be a big board menu at the back.

Marlon *is in the office, visible through the window, wearing a big coat, sitting working at the computer, maybe with his back to us.*

The play begins when **Damon** *comes in, looks round and starts clearing up with obvious reluctance. His methods are cack-handed. Maybe at first picking up odd plates or bottles, taking them one at a time to the counter. As he gets fed up with his slow progress, he could go to the other extreme and try to pick up too much so that he is dangerously overloaded. During this,* **Marlon** *gets up and comes out of the office and stands at the edge of the mezzanine obviously bemused by* **Damon***.*

Marlon   What's the game?

Damon   Oh my sweet fuck!

Damon *almost drops the dishes. By the time he has recovered and is standing struggling to hold them all,* **Marlon** *has joined him and is standing looking at him.*

Damon   Didny see you there, big man. Didny even see you, know what I mean?

Marlon   What's the game exactly?

Damon   My da pure asked us to help out, before the course and that.

Marlon   Well, take less.

Damon   What?

Marlon   Try taking less.

Damon   Just getting a move on till I catch my bus. Got to head up town there as soon as. Know what I mean?

Marlon looks at **Damon** *and goes to go.* **Damon** *carries on moving the dishes.* **Marlon** *thinks better of it and stops in his tracks.*

Marlon   What course?

Damon *almost drops the dishes again.*

Damon   Oh ya big wet shite, ye.

He recovers.

Marlon   No course scheduled for this weekend.

Damon   Must of totally got it arse over tit, my da must of.

Marlon *goes to go.* **Damon** *carries on with dishes.* **Marlon** *stops in his tracks.*

Marlon   At least you've got some go in you.

Damon *almost drops the dishes again. This time more perilously.*

Damon   Aw, cunting cunting fuck, man. What?

Marlon   Unlike that son of mine.

Damon   Aw, Ronan's a good guy. Excellent guy, Ronan. Superb.

Marlon   Excellent at what? Superb at what exactly?

Damon Going through a wee stage – the Ronan boy – till he gets his shit together!

Marlon Join the business, wash the dishes, work his way up? No shame there. Take a stand against everything I stand for? Be something. Or at least pick up half a dozen tarts and shag them into oblivion. Perfectly acceptable behaviour. If only.

Damon Be a lucky cunt if he could shag half a dozen tarts into oblivion. Wouldny mind shagging a half-dozen tarts myself, if you've got any going spare. 'Shagging them into oblivion', man, know what I mean?

Marlon Not two words together. Not two. Unless he's at it. Posing. Away in film-star fantasyland. Well, no more. It's get a life or get to fuck out!

Marlon *looks at* **Damon** *to see if he's impressed with his firmness and turn of phrase.* **Damon** *looks blank.* **Marlon** *turns suddenly and goes out.* **Damon** *goes to continue with the dishes, but thinks better of it and watches* **Marlon** *go right off this time.*

Damon *blithely carries on and immediately trips and drops the lot.*

Damon Aw, fuckin fuckin fuckin fuck! Fuckin fuckin fuckin fuck! Fuckin fuckin fuckin fuckin fuckin . . . !

He starts clearing up.

Aw, fuck it!

He gives up and makes himself a coffee and takes some food and goes and sits down. He just begins to relax when **Ringo** *comes in.*

Ringo Aw, fuckin fuckin fuckin fuckin shithole. (*Seeing* **Damon**.) Did I not ask you to lend a hand, son? You could of at least got started.

Damon Cool it, my man. The big guy comes in. He's like: There's no course on, nothing.

Ringo Well, there isny one.

Damon But you're like: get all that shit in there to fuck.

Ringo   Isny an actual course. Ronan boy's rigged one up so he can get some wee tart down here, shag her stupid.

Damon   Is Ronan gonny shag some wee tart?

Ringo   Slip it right up her, he will. Right up her wee lulu. Till she sings, the wee guy.

Damon   Should of totally told his da, the boy. His da totally thinks Ronan's a pure knobhead.

Damon *goes to go.*

Ringo   Where you away to?

Damon   Call round see a few of the guys, up the town, da. See the old dear. Bit of cash up to her.

Ringo   Giving cash to that cunty old crab for?

Damon   Pure phoned us up and asked us, my ma.

Ringo   Give her fuck all bar a boot in the snatch. Old alkie.

Damon   Button it, gonny. Old man pure slagging off the old dear. Isny right that caper. End up getting a pure trauma o'er the heid of it, me. I'm heading.

Damon *goes to go.* **Ringo** *calls after him.*

Ringo   You getting this cash from, son?

Damon   That's for me to know.

Ringo   Not flogging tablets, are you?

Damon   Know what I mean?

Ringo   Urny, are you?

Damon   Gonny stop me?

Ringo   Course no, son. I'm a good da to you. Rape, violent robbery, racially aggravated assault? Your every action gets my full support. But if you're flogging tablets you couldny slip your old man a few notes, could you?

Damon Get to fuck.

Ringo Goin' ya tube, ye. Hope some cunt shags you up the arse.

Damon So do I hope some cunt shags me up the arse. As long as it's no you.

Damon *goes.*

Ringo (*aside*) Does your old heart good to hear that, does it no? Takes after his old man, the boy. Tight cunt!

Ringo *carries on clearing up and disappears behind counter or into cupboard.*

Whitney *comes in. Looks round, shakes her head.*

Whitney For fuck's sake.

She starts picking things up at random. She finds a set of false teeth in a bowl of nachos, a pair of sodden knickers in a glass, a tampon in an ashtray and a used condom in a cup. She bins each in turn and **Ringo** *comes in to find her holding up the condom. They clear up as they talk.*

Ringo Who's doing the training?

Whitney The mug, as per usual. An' if I had my way there wouldny be any training. The future's with the franchise. Owning the brand, no the branches is where it's at. Mean, I'm totally like that to O'Donnell: gonny let some other cunt do the work. Gonny let some other cunt do the *worrying.* Gonny, for fuck's sake, *embrace the Zeitgeist.* O'Donnell's like that: till you're global you've not got a brand. I'm like that: we've totally saturated the St Eunuch Centre with branches, we've just shifted the whole entire HQ from Monknock to London and we've totally, totally bent Brazil o'er a barrel so we can get their beans off them for buttons, is that no global enough? He's like that: you're nobody till you've broken into Broadway. When you've made it in Manhattan, then you've gone global.

Ringo   All this palaver pretending there's a course just so the boy can shag a slag!

Whitney   But he doesny shag them: *they* shag *him*.

Ringo   How do you work that out?

Whitney   Seemingly he's always been trying to say to them: 'I'm looking for love.' But his stutter kept getting in the road.

Ringo   He telt you that?

Whitney   Aye!

Ringo   How did he manage to get the words out?

Whitney   Because he's went an' invested in breathing lessons!

Ringo   Breathing lessons, my arse. Breathing's not his problem. Wouldny be alive if he wasny breathing. Not breathing lessons he should be getting. It's lessons in not stuttering. Stuttery wee cunt, that he is. Who'd want a son like that? Bring shame to you a stutter like that. No wonder O'Donnell's off his chump, having to listen to all that stuttering morning, noon and night. On and on and on. Stutter, stutter, stutter. Something should be done, Whitney.

Whitney   Something has been done, Ringo. Must of practised saying 'I totally love you, doll' o'er a hunner times in the last week alone.

Ringo   So what's the course for? He can just tell her he totally loves her. End of problem.

Whitney   Aye, but it isny. Turns out this wee lassie – Celine's her name – she works in with Mick at the Suckingcock Street branch. Ronan totally saw her through the window, so he did and's totally lost the heid o'er the heid o' her. But Mick says Celine's totally in love with this other guy, Jarvis. So I've decided you're gonny get this Jarvis down here an' a.

Ringo   What the fuck fer?

Whitney   So we can put him an' Celine oft each another, ya tube.

Ringo   Aye, but how am I gonny get him to do that?

Whitney   Well, you're dead intelligent, so you are.

Ringo   So if I'm intelligent, can I plop my knob into your slippy wee snatch? I don't like to ask, only I totally love ye an' you've got a smashing big arse on you.

Whitney (*regretfully*)   I couldny, Ringo.

Ringo   How no?

Whitney   Because you totally turn my stomach. But it's nothing personal. Mean, you know what I'm like: totally loss the heid when I get my hauns on mountains ay flesh. Tell you what: put on three stones and I'll let you see my knockers.

Ringo   I've tried everything, Whitney. I eat all the shit I can get my hands on and shit it straight back out again. An' you let O'Donnell shag you.

Whitney   O'Donnell pays my wages, you prick.

They carry on clearing up.

Ronan *comes in, unseen, and doesn't know what to do. When he stutters it should be extremely painful to listen to because he's trying so hard not to.*

Ronan   Is?/ Um ah. Um ah. Um ah. Um ah.

Ringo *and* **Whitney** *turn to find him.*

Ringo   In the name of fuck.

Ronan   I ah/ I ah/

Ringo   Your old man shelling out on lessons and you're as shite as ever!

Ronan   Um ah. Um ah. Ah/

Whitney   Just do your breathing and take your time.
(Shut the fuck up, you!)

Ronan *stops to breathe and concentrate for a second. Then he
snatches a bit of breath between each word.*

Ronan   ... Is ... she ... here ... yet?

Ringo   Oh, you've got to be joking. Celine'll totally freak
out when she hears that.

Whitney   Ignore him. An' she's no here yet. But she'll go
apeshite about you. (Ya bastard.)

Ringo   Aw, face facts, Whitney, uh? (*exaggerates*) 'Is ... she
... here ... yet?' I've heard more shaggable daleks.

Whitney   Just try again. Imagine I'm her. Tell her exactly
what you think of her. Just breathe first and a tiny wee bit
smoother maybe.

Ronan (*big effort*)   I eh ... I eh ... You eh ... You eh ...
(*Sails into American.*) You're my dream come true, you know.
You're so cute. Ever since I first saw you I can't stop
thinking about you. I'm Brad! ... I eh ... I eh ... Sorry!

Ringo   Aye, it's all very well pittin' her off Jarvis. But what
aboot when the knobheid here opens his gob an' undoes a'
yer work?

Whitney   Can you no build him up, ya clown, instead ay?

Ringo's *mobile goes. He takes it out and answers it.*

Ringo (*to phone*)   Yo! ... Right ... Oh right ... Be right
down.

He switches phone off and puts it away.

That's her here and totally raging.

Ronan   I ah ... I ah ... I/

Whitney   Right: show her to her room. Simmer her
down. Tell her you're her staff. You'll do anything for her.
Then get her into the uniform, bring her up.

Ringo *goes to go.*

Whitney   And tell Britney I want to see her!

Ringo *goes.*

Ronan   I ah . . . I ah . . .

Whitney   Ye've just to remember you're drap-deid handsome, horny as fuck and totally, totally loaded. Be her that's nervous, no you!

Ronan   Oh, but . . . I ah . . . I ah/

Whitney   Just breathe, Ronan. Mind an' breathe.

Ronan   I . . . don't . . . want . . . her . . . to . . . know . . . I'm . . . rich.

Whitney   But you are rich. You can't hide that. You being rich is the best thing about you.

Ronan   I ah/ . . . I ah/

Whitney   Breathe now.

Ronan   I . . . might . . . give . . . the . . . money . . . up.

Whitney *(almost screaming)*   You can't. You don't mean it. Mean: why would you do that?

Ronan   Because . . . it's . . . my . . . father's . . . money.

Whitney   Oh my fuck! Oh my Christ! Why didn't you say so before?

Ronan   Because . . . of . . . my eh/ my eh/ my/

Whitney *(whispering tenderly)*   Breathe.

Ronan *(big effort)*   Because . . . of . . . my . . . stutter.

Whitney *is silenced by this enormous revelation.*

Marlon *comes in and goes straight to luggage.*

Marlon   That's the car ready. I'm out of time. And so are you.

Ronan   I ah/ I ah/

Marlon   Costly Coffee is about to enter a new era. And so are you.

Ronan   Um ah/ Um ah/ Um ah/

Marlon   Just as Costly will need clear aims, objectives, plans of action, targets and constant self-monitoring, so will you.

Ronan   Ah/ Ah/ Ah/

Marlon   Costly are having to look out to embrace the globe in future and so will you. Just as Costly are cutting loose from government handouts and hellhole Monknock, you're cutting free from my handouts and the hell of indecision. Just as there will be no more prevarication, no more passengers and no more stuttering for Costly, there won't be for you either. Well, what do you say?

Ronan   Oh I/ I ah/ I/

Ronan *runs up to office.*

Marlon *bursts into tears.*

Whitney   Don't take it like that.

Marlon   It's just I/ I/ I love that boy so much. And if this doesn't work out I/ I/

Whitney   But it's so obvious you love him! And marvellous to see it: a truly loving dad being hard on his arsehole of a backsliding son. He'll thank you for it one day.

Marlon   Only I've never actually told him I love him. And all the experts: they're now saying/

Whitney   And all the experts are wrong. A' the ones that get on in the world, what do you think they're doing it for? They're totally looking for the love they never got as children.

Marlon   I'd hate to die without him knowing!

Whitney   What are you talking about dying for? OK.
You've got a wee heart condition on ye but it willny kill ye.
Oh no. You totally did the right thing by your boy being
hard with him. An' you were the king ay hard, by the way.
And you canny be hard enough in my book.

They kiss.

Whitney   You're really and truly actually gonny buy up
the whole entire 307 branches of the Coffee Company of
America?

Marlon   Looks like it.

Whitney   All that investment going out your bank
account, all that ownership, all that stress. An' you wi' your
heart condition. Ye'll end up killin' yersel'.

Marlon   I know. I know. But I have been thinking about
what you said about franchising. So when I get back I think
I might have a little surprise for you.

Whitney   Oh, ya big bastard, ye. Be in agony all weekend
if you don't tell me.

Marlon   Would you rather I told you now?

Whitney   Don't you dare. Always leave a woman
screaming for more. And you do, by the way, big man. You
certainly do.

Marlon *goes to kiss her.*

Britney (*from off*)   Whitney? It's Britney. I've been telt to
look for ye. Where the fuck are you?

Whitney (*shouting off*)   Here I'm, Britney. (*To* **Marlon**.)
You go before my wee sister comes and nabs you, ya dirty
big ride, you.

Marlon *goes to kiss her.*

Whitney   No, big man. No. On you go now. (*Aside.*) Never
live it down if the cow walks in on us.

Marlon *picks up his bags and goes.* **Whitney** *waves him goodbye as* **Britney** *comes in.*

Britney   Here I'm, Whitney. What is it?

Whitney   C'mere, Britney. Till I see you right.

Britney   Och, take as long as you want. Feast your eyes.

Whitney   You going up the town looking like that?

Britney   What's wrong with me?

Whitney   Cover yourself up!

Britney   I paid good money for this tan!

Whitney   You'll give me a showing-up. Get yourself covered.

Britney (*puts on her little jacket*)   I hate you. What are you making me feel like shite for? I'm your wee sister.

Whitney   That's better. You're so gorgeous, you, when you want to be. Look at you. Standing there in your full-on no tits, no pubes, underage glory.

Britney   That's what the guys are always telling me.

Whitney (*playing up to her*)   What do you say to them, Britney?

Britney   I never brag about my looks, for a start. No, I usually just say: 'I'm just very, very lucky to be so good-looking. I could have ended up like my sister, Whitney.'

Whitney (*aside*)   Well, she would be gorgeous. Only you can't see her face for her mouth. It's like a toilet. Perfect for guys to piss into. (*To* **Britney**.) So do you like guys moving in on you or what?

Britney   It's my drug!

Whitney   Could you get some twat to get off with you?

Britney   I get guys to get off with me every day of the week.

Whitney   So will you get a guy to get off with you for me, Britney?

Britney   When?

Whitney   Bit later on. I'll call you when he's here.

Britney   Better no be long though, Whitney, right? I'm going up the town, shopping.

Whitney   What shops ye going intae?

Britney   HIV Music maybe.

Whitney   You gonny pick up some CDs?

Britney   No, I'm urny. I've got no money.

Whitney   So you're no going shopping?

Britney   I am so going shopping.

Whitney   How do you work that out?

Britney   I'm going into shops, amen't I?

Whitney   How come you've not got any money?

Britney   Because you invite me all the way down to this dump to stay the night because you miss me. And yet you totally never give me any fuckin money, ya miserable cow, ye.

Whitney   So what about if I give you some money for CDs?

Britney   Get to fuck. What would I want money for CDs for?

Whitney   Why wouldn't you?

Britney   Because I've got all the CDs I want!

Whitney   So what are you going into HIV music for?

Britney   To go shopping, Whitney! Are you not listening to me? (*Aside.*) I must of been pure at the back of the queue when they were handing out the big sisters!

Whitney   Do you want money for anything else then?

Britney   Well, I've got fuck all to wear for a start.

Whitney (*aside*)   Aye and nothing's what she usually wears. (*To* **Britney**.) Where from?

Britney   I could get something nice out of Greatgirl. Or maybe even out of CNUT. CNUT's stuff's no bad.
[*Pronounce as seanut.*]

Celine (*off*)   We nearly there yet? Like a fuckin maze this place.

Ringo (*off*)   Just round here.

Ronan *comes out on to mezzanine.*

Britney   Is that him there?

Whitney   No, that's not him.

Britney   Och, Whitney. How can it no be him? Pure ride so he is.

Ronan   I ah/ I ah/

Britney   Aw, he's no got a stutter, has he? Looks a bit of a wank anyway. Ugly. Call me right? I pure hate guys with stutters.

Britney *goes.*

Celine (*off*)   Better be just round here, that's all I can say. I'm going home if it isny.

Whitney *goes upstairs and into office, gesturing* **Ronan** *to follow.* **Ringo** *lingers on the mezzanine to watch.* **Celine**, *in uniform, comes in with* **Ringo**.

Ringo   Och, gonny just tune into us for one minute, Celine.

Celine   You are so far up my nose.

Ringo   All your ranting and raving! Mean: what's it for?

Celine   I'll tell you what it's for. Up at the crack of dawn just so's to be on time, supposed to be. I wouldny of minded but I didny even get to shag my Jarvis or nothing first! Then you're like: 'Get into your uniform, Celine, you're late.' In we come – rushing like fuck, by the way – and after all that there's no even any other cunt here yet. And I've been accosted. That's what it's for!

Whitney *nips out of the office and pulls in the dreaming* **Ronan**.

Ringo   Och, you've not been accosted.

Celine   Don't you contradict me. If I say I've been accosted, I've been accosted. Only been working in the Suckingcock Street branch five days and already it's 'Get your coat on. You're going to Monknock Castle for the weekend to get your management training.' Mean I'm totally like that to Mick: 'What do I want management training for? I'm only working at Costly pure temporary, so I'm are.' He's like that: 'Everybody at Costly's got to get their management training. It's the rules.' I'm like that: totally needing the money. Mean, what choice have I got? So see you, Ringo? Your negative vibes are doing my nut in.

Ringo   I just don't get it with you, Celine. So Ronan O'Donnell, right? Hunky son of the owner of Costly Coffee wants to meet you and you're not interested? Who the fuck do you think you are?

Celine   Your values are in your arse: people like you. I don't care if Ronan O'Donnell's hunky and owns the whole entire planet! And what's he want to meet me for?

Ringo   Oh, fuck knows. Maybe likes you or something!

Celine   Well, I don't like him.

Ringo   Well, could you not fake liking him? You canny knock back an opportunity like that!

Celine   They call me Celine McAnespie and I say it like it is! If a guy's a dug, I tell him he's a dug. And how can he like me?

Ringo   How *can't* he?

Celine   Hasny even met me.

Ringo   Aye, but he'll've heard about you.

Celine   Heard what about me?

Ringo   I don't know. Heard you're gorgeous or something.

Celine   Am I fuck gorgeous.

Ringo   Well, I'd ride you.

Celine   Well, *I* wouldny ride *you*. Och, I'm heading.

Celine *takes her uniform off and dumps it. She is wearing T-shirt and jeans. The T-shirt should say CNUT front and back.*

Ringo   What do you think you're doing?

Celine   Taking off my honking stinking uniform off. What do you think I'm doing?

Ringo   And what's that you've got on?

Celine   What's wrong with what I've got on?

Ringo   What's right with it? You've got words on your tits!

Celine   That's my good CNUT T-shirt, you.

Ringo   Aye and what's a seanut exactly? No such thing as a seanut. Seanut! What's the world coming to, that's all I can say! Seanut! What do you do when you go to the pictures? Ask for a bag of seanuts? I'd get that off if I was you. And totally knocks your knockers all out of shape, by the way. Seanut! You get fish in the sea, no nuts! Seanut. What next?

Celine   You're gonny get flattened is what's next! You're as bad as wee Rita, my ex-pal. Pals for years her and me, so we were. Went everywhere together. Every Saturday night for donkeys – before I met my boyfriend Jarvis – you'd see us wearing wur CNUT T-shirts at the Shag Shack Club. Then this time she suggests going to Club Arty for a change. So she's like that: mind and get dressed up. So OK, I take her at her word an' totally go oot an' buy brand new CNUT T-shirt and jeans and meet her outside Club Arty. Right away she's like that: 'Fuck do you think you're wearing, Celine? I'm no cruising round Club Arty with a creep in a CNUT T-shirt. You'll make a cunt out of me.'

She goes to go.

Ringo   Hey, wait wait wait wait a wee minute first. What's your job title?

Celine   Assistant manager, how?

Ringo   And how much do you get paid?

Celine   Three pounds an hour, how?

Ringo   First job, I suppose?

Celine   First job was assistant manager at Cute Clothing.

Ringo   How come you left?

Celine   They sacked me for knocking stuff.

Ringo   What did you say when they caught you?

Celine   I said: 'I thought you were supposed to knock stuff.'

Ringo   You what?

Celine   Well, it was before the minimum wage came in. I thought you were meant to knock stuff to make up your wages.

Ringo   What was your next job?

Celine   Assistant manager at Rave Reads.

Ringo   Did you get sacked for knocking the books, I suppose?

Celine   Oh no. They said I was getting sacked for being cheeky to customers.

Ringo   And were you?

Celine   No! All I ever was to customers was totally one hundred per cent honest.

Ringo   What did you actually say to them?

Celine   Usually just something like: 'How can youse lot read all those fuckin books? Do my nut in, so it would. They're totally boring.'

Ringo   And did you have another job after that?

Celine   Aye. One more. Assistant manager at Best Burgers. That's how I met my Jarvis.

Ringo   What did they sack you for?

Celine   The manager caught me giving Jarvis a blow job in the back shop.

Ringo   What did he sack you for that for?

Celine   Because the manager'd just asked me for a blow job and I'd said: no, sorry, I've got a sore mouth.

Ringo   And did you?

Celine   Did I what?

Ringo   Did you have a sore mouth?

Celine   Aye, I had a sore mouth. Are you calling me a liar?

Ringo   So what did you give Jarvis a blow job for with a sore mouth?

Celine   Because I'm so in love with him it's freaky. Why do you think?

Ringo   So what's this Jarvis got that Ronan's not got? Is he gorgeous?

Celine   No. Is he fuck. He's a fat ugly bastard and he's got a wee knob.

Ringo   Does he no satisfy you?

Celine   When did a wee knob ever satisfy anybody?

Ringo   Is he rich?

Celine   Get to fuck. They pay washers at Best Burgers.

Ringo   So what do you see in him?

Celine   Och. You canny put it into words. He's got/ He's got/ Well, he's got actual principles. It's principles, principles, principles with him. Aye, principles coming out his arse! An', see, if a guy's totally for something or totally against something: I totally get erect nipples and a soaking wet pussy.

Ringo   This isny real. Must be something about him you don't like.

Celine   Of course there's something about him I don't like.

Ringo   What's that?

Celine   He's a greedy bastard. But he's going on a diet soon as he packs in Best Burgers. Well, he canny exactly go on a diet working in among a' they burgers.

Ringo   So what's he working at Best Burgers for if it makes a fat cunt ay him?

Celine   He's researching the workplace practices of a typical junk-food multinational.

Ringo   So he prefers stuffing his face to stuffing you, he's the size of a house and he bores the face of you talking shite about sweet fuck all and you're still into him?

Celine   Yes, I am still into him. What of it?

Ringo   This three pounds an hour malarkey is what of it. It's eating your brains is what of it. Whereas if you totally stick in and do your management training you get your own shop and as well also fantastic Costly manager's perks and fantastic Costly manager's pay ay six pounds an hour.

Celine   Six pounds an hour?

Ringo   Six pounds an hour.

Celine   Jesus fucking God. But I couldny do it. I totally promised Jarvis I'd only compromise myself working at Costly for a few months till I got back on my feet. Six pounds an hour, all the same? I'd be rich. But no. I couldny stick it here with that creep Ronan O'Donnell sniffing around me all weekend. He's a creep.

Ringo   Have you seen him?

Celine   No, I haven't seen him.

Ringo   So how do you know he's a creep?

Celine   Because he accosted me!

Ringo   Aye, but it was with the highly romantic intention of shagging you. No of shagging you, I mean. I mean, it was with the highly romantic intention of no shagging you. Well, he did want to shag you. But no right away. Because he had the highly romantic intention of telling you he loves you and asking you if you'd mind waiting till your second date before he shagged you.

Celine   There's to be zero tolerance of romantic intentions! Comes anywhere near me with his romantic intentions he'll get his balls boiled. Wanting to shag me and he hasn't even seen me!

Ringo   He has seen you!

Celine   Where?

Ringo   Och, I don't know.

Celine   Where's he seen me?

Ringo   I don't know, I'm telling you.

Celine   Could someone please tell me what's going on? It's like he's found some old shot of me with my tits out on the internet personal columns when I was desperate before I met my boyfriend Jarvis. And he's like that: 'No her. No her. Her!'

Ringo   Och, he didny look you up on the internet.

Celine   Where did he see me then?

Ringo   I don't know, I'm telling you.

Celine   Right, I'm definitely heading!

Celine *goes to go.*

Ringo   He seen you through the window of the Suckingcock Street branch ay Costly Coffee.

Celine   Looking at people through windows? That is so sick! Must be a total perv! Mean, if he's seen me how can't he at least come up and talk to me?

Ringo   He's shy.

Celine   Aye fly, you mean.

Ringo   He'll be makin' sure you like him first.

Celine   He's got to take his chances like everyone else. He's got to give you the option of telling him to fuck off to his face! Is he a wimp?

Ringo   It's his upbringing. He's had no previous experience of having to give people options. He'll not realise he has the option of giving you the option.

Celine   Is someone paying you to talk pish?

Ringo   You're too much, you. Out of an entire population of highly shaggable totty Ronan O'Donnell picks you out as his choice to get fired into and you're saying no?

Celine   This is one piece of highly shaggable totty that likes a bit of consultation on who gets to fire into her. I'll just stick with Jarvis!

Celine *starts to go.* **Ringo** *signals desperately to* **Whitney** *to send* **Ronan** *down.* **Ronan** *comes down towards the end of* **Ringo***'s speech.*

Ringo   At least wait till you see Ronan first. Mean: what a sight that boy is. Sunray on a daily basis. Not a plook in sight. Face that gorgeous he could be mistook for a poof. Buttocks of steel. Pecs like a pair of big shiny fish. Massive knob. Hard-ons on demand. Day and night service. And see the words coming out his gob: every one of them's poetry. Mean, face it: if he was a creep, he'd've walked into the Suckingcock Street branch, pulled you into the toilets, had your knickers at your ankles and been inside you before you can say: 'Pass the condoms.'

Celine   Total loser you, by the way.

She makes to go again and walks right into **Ronan**. *Very long pause as* **Ronan** *and* **Celine** *are frozen, looking at each other.* **Ringo** *hesitates and then is waved away by* **Whitney**. *He quietly goes up to the office. The movement quietly breaks the pause and* **Celine** *and* **Ronan** *are forced to look away.* **Ronan** *breaks away and* **Celine** *is first to look back. From now on* **Ronan** *finds direct eye contact extremely difficult. At some point in the scene* **Ringo** *might be seen through the office window discreetly taking out a bit of paper and making a phone call.*

Celine   Hiya . . . I said hiya . . . Eh, excuse me: have you got an actual voice on you or what?

Ronan *looks at her with difficulty, tries to smile and very quickly looks away again.*

Celine   You can look at me if you like . . . I don't bite . . . Unless you ask me first.

Ronan *doesn't know what to do and on impulse heads behind the counter, much to the mystification of* **Celine**. *By pointing and gesturing, he suggests food and coffee to* **Celine**. *Bewildered, she finds herself nodding and agreeing. He pours coffee. Suddenly she realises something.*

Celine   I've totally got it now. I'm so sorry, by the way. Celine makes a tit of herself again! Ha ha. You're deif, aren't you? Deif and dumb?

Ronan (*horrified*)   Oh no/ I eh/ I eh/

Celine   Oh, it's all right. You don't have to speak nor nothing. You just chat away at me with your wee signs and I'll work it out.

Ronan *is frustrated by the continuation of the misunderstanding. But he is calmed by the urgent need to speak being relieved. He brings over her food and gives it to her.*

Celine   Aw, thanks. You're ace, so you are.

Ronan *beams shyly.*

Celine   And lovely place, isn't it?

He nods eagerly.

Dead, dead realistic. Mean, it's only a training centre. You wouldny think they'd go to all that bother of making it look real. Mean, that's actual coffee you've given me. Actual coffee and a actual croissant. No bad either. Considering it's Costly. Ha ha. Mean, hope they're better to you than they are to me.

Ronan *begins to get alarmed and it increases as* **Celine** *speaks.*

Celine   Bastards forced me to come here today, you know. Forced. Accosted actually. And it turns out that they're just trying to get me off with Ronan. That's the son, by the way. What a creep. Stalking me seemingly. Looking in at me at my work. I'm at the Suckingcock Street shop. Which shop are you from? Oh, and what's your name?

Ronan *hesitates, then goes to go out.* **Celine** *panics and stops him by grabbing his shoulder. He turns and she lets go.*

Celine   Did I say something wrong or what? Didny mean to put you off nor nothing. No, you just stay, why don't you?

Mean, Ronan willny likely want to get off with you. Ha ha.
Though you never know. Ha ha.

Ronan *tries to smile.*

A long pause when he has difficulty returning her gaze.

Celine   What is it? Is there something wrong?

Ronan   I eh/ I eh/ (*Into American.*) Everything's fine.
Thought maybe you could stick around a while. Hang out,
you know?

Celine *looks at him in amazement.* **Whitney** *comes out of the office
and stands on the mezzanine.* **Ringo** *appears at the office doorway.*
Whitney *watches the following with mounting despair.* **Celine**
suddenly works it out.

Celine   You *can* speak!

Ronan   Sure can.

Celine   You've been totally taking the mick, you wee
prick.

Ronan   Oh no, I/

Celine   Don't oh no me. You've been totally ripping the
pish out of deif dumb stuttery people.

Ronan   I eh/ I eh/

Celine   No, don't try and get out of it. They deif dumb
stuttery people have got a hard enough job to gain
acceptance into society.

Ronan   Oh no, ma'am! It's just that I've got issues, you
know?

Celine   What issues have you got?

Ronan   Introvert extrovert issues. So until I get to know
people I can be/ be/

Celine   Backward at coming forward?

Ronan   Exactly!

Celine   Me too! Aye, believe it or not, me too! So what are you doing in Scotland? You're not/ You/ You didny come all this way to learn how to manage a coffee shop?

Ronan   Sure did. Well, it seems that Costly Coffee is one of the biggest and best in the business? Is that your impression?

Celine   No, it is not my impression!

Ronan   You're kidding me!

Celine   I am not kidding you. But don't ask me to explain it or nothing. All I know is that my/ my/ my good pal Jarvis says/ And Jarvis is like a total world expert on what's wrong with Costly Coffee. You can ask him if you ever get to meet him.

Ronan   I might just do that, miss.

Celine   And don't call me miss. I'm Celine. Who are you?

Ronan   Well I'm eh/ I'm eh, Brad.

Whitney *puts on a T-shirt and comes downstairs.*

Celine   Very pleased to meet you. Oh who's this?

As **Whitney** *comes forward, the T-shirt falls into place. It says 'Costly Coffee Goes Global'.*

Whitney   Welcome to Costly Management training course. I'm your tutor, Whitney. Pleased to meet youse both. You'll be Celine?

Celine   That's right.

Whitney   You Brad?

Ronan   Sure am, miss.

Whitney   Ony questions?

Celine   Is it just the two of us?

Whitney   Aye. Because ye get a quality ane oan ane training wi' Costly. Now, where's your uniforms?

Celine *finds herself putting her uniform back on.*

Whitney   I know where yours'll be, Brad. 'Mon, I'll show ye!

Whitney *signals* **Ringo** *to come down as she goes out with* **Ronan**. **Ringo** *comes down.*

Ringo   Nice guy that Brad, eh?

Celine   What?

Ringo   Ye get on with him OK?

Celine   Aye, I got on with him. What of it?

Ringo   I'm just saying/

Celine   I heard what you said. But what I want to know is: why did ye say it? I totally told you I'm seeing Jarvis, Ringo. Mean: I don't even know anything about Brad. No bad-looking, I'll give you that. And the Yank accent's a total turn-on. But I didny even get the chance to find oot if he's got any principles. And besides he's deif, dumb and stuttery hauf the time. Couldny stick all that stuttering. End up nutting the cunt, so I would. Then that mad cow Whitney totally rushing him out to put on his uniform. And he just go totally goes wi' her. Like a wimp. Aye, youse are all the same at Costly Coffee. Totally getting up people's noses.

She takes the uniform back off and dumps it.

Ringo   Why would I want to get up your nose, Celine, I'm your staff.

Celine   You're my what?

Ringo   I'm your staff, I'm telling you.

Celine   What do I want staff for?

Ringo   All I've been told is I'm your staff.

Celine   OK. So if you're my staff, could you get out my way till I get out of this dump?

She goes to go.

Ringo   You can't just go like that. I'll have to phone down to the gates first to get them to let you out. And I'll have to get a driver up an' a'.

Celine   I'll just walk.

Ringo   You canny just walk.

Celine   How no?

Ringo   You're in the grounds of an actual castle. And it's totally stowed out with antiques. So there's dugs and patrols and perimeter fencing and it's a couple of miles. Did you no notice on your way in? Too busy roaring and greeting for your Jarvis, were you?

Celine   They'll just have to shoot me. I'm heading. How much did you say they pay managers?

Ringo   Six pounds an hour.

Celine   In the name of fuck. That's worth thinking about. But not till I talk to Jarvis first and ask him if he minds. *Six* pound an hour? Och, I'm heading. If I try to get out of here, will they set their big dugs on me? Six pounds an hour? Och fuck it. I'm going home, dugs or no dugs. Six pounds is a fuckofa lot, all the same. But I don't care. I'm goin' home tae Jarvis.

Ringo   There's no point in you going home to Jarvis.

Celine   How no?

Ringo   Because he's coming here to you.

Celine   What are you talking about? He's away on a protest at Monknock village. Is that near here?

Ringo   Aye, it is. Two miles down the road!

Celine   Oh my fuck. When's he arriving?

Ringo   Ten minutes.

Celine   You have totally got to be jokin', man. An' what happened tae the protest?

Ringo   It's been called off.

Celine   How come?

Ringo   He didny say.

Celine   But how does he know where I am? And how do you know he knows where I am?

Ringo   I phoned him up and told him.

Celine   What for?

Ringo   Because you've been roaring and greeting for him all morning.

Celine   How did you get his number?

Ringo   Out your bag.

Celine   You went into my bag?

Ringo   Well, you were in the toilet crying your eyes out. 'I want my Jarvis. I want my ma.'

Celine   You leave my wee ma out of it. My wee ma's my best pal in the whole wide world. And you can't go into my bag. Jarvis is coming here?

Ringo   Aye, Celine.

Celine   You're my staff. Here?

Ringo   Aye, I says.

Celine   I don't let my staff go into my bag. Catch you in my bag again, you're sacked. My Jarvis is actually coming here! My Jarvis! My wee big Jarvis! Yes! Oh he's only a bloke, I know. But we've got so much in common. All but identical bank balances. Fuck all in them. And he's an actual assistant manager too. And it's like totally amazing how we'll meet after work, walk down the street the first person we pass is like: 'How's it going, doll?' To me! Then the next one's like: 'All right, wee man?' To him! Not to mention we've also got totally similar interests. I mean, practically every one of our conversations is about how we're totally freaked out with love for each another. So, see, if you're lying and he doesn't turn up sharpish you can go to hell and don't come back. And stop calling me Celine. If you're my staff it's Miss McAnespie to you!

Celine *goes to go.*

Ringo   Where are you going now?

Celine   Canny let Jarvis see me looking like this, can I?

Ringo   How no?

Celine   Because he'll totally call me a label-wearing victim of multinational advertising an' say I'm just trying to get people to like me.

Ringo   What's wrong wi' getting people to like you?

Celine   It's against Jarvis's principles getting people to like you.

Celine *goes as* **Whitney** *comes back in with* **Ronan**.

Whitney   Where's Celine?

Ringo   She's wanting to look her best for Jarvis coming.

Ronan   I ah/ I ah/

Whitney   Mind and breathe, Ronan, son.

Ronan   I ah/ I ah/ (*Bewildered and angry, to* **Ringo**.) What's . . . he . . . coming . . . here . . . for?

Whitney   Well, how the fuck are we gonny put Celine off Jarvis if Jarvis isny here for us to put her off?

Ringo   Aye, this Jarvis one'll be in here tongue straight down the back of Celine's giant gob, one hand round the back rubbing her unbelievable arse, other one up the front and right into her fascinating fanny somewhere.

Ronan I ah/ I ah/

Ringo Unless we put a stop to it first.

Ronan I . . . don't . . . want . . . you . . . to . . . put . . . him . . . off.

Ringo Well, what dae ye want?

Ronan I want us to just like totally fall in love, you know?

Ringo Fuck's he talking about now? 'Love'? Should have a stop pit tae it. A' this love wank! 'Love'! Should be giein' slags a boot in the snatch, no fallin' in love wi' them. 'Love'! Aye, if it's love ye want, away tae Paris, ya tube. This is Scotland ye're in: we don't dae love here!

Whitney (*aside to* **Ringo**) Can you no help build up his confidence? (*She gives* **Ringo** *a quick, promising fondle.*)

Ringo Tell you what, son. She thinks your Yank accent's a total turn-on. An' your massive knob'll stand you in good stead. Seemingly, Celine canny get any satisfaction out of Jarvis.

Ronan Cool!

His mobile goes off. He takes it out and listens.

(*To phone.*) Be right down. (*To others.*) He's here.

He goes.

Ronan I ah/ I ah/

Britney (*off*) Right, Whitney. I'm totally bored of waiting. Is he no here yet?

Whitney (*to* **Ronan**) You go up and wait. An' practise your breathing.

Ronan *goes upstairs as* **Britney** *comes on.*

Britney Where is he?

Whitney Gonny give Jarvis a minute to get in the door.

Britney   Aye, but what've I say to him?

Whitney   Well, don't start asking him if he likes the size ay yer tits?

Britney   What else is there to talk about except the size ay me tits?

Whitney   It's more what you're not to talk about.

Britney   What have I not to talk about?

Whitney   Anything you normally talk about! And don't go being like what you're normally like either.

Britney   What am I normally like?

Whitney   What are you not normally like? Well, for a start there's the bimbo with the attention span shorter than a eunuch's knob. Get her to fuck. And her with the tongue would cut open metal. Don't go there, girl. Then the butter-wouldn't-melt-never-been-fucked act. Cut the crap. And as for the nightclub poser. I get a beamer just thinking about it. The tossers you go for can't get enough of it. But the weirdo you've to get to work on – this Jarvis – he'd blow all that shit away.

Britney (*not understanding*)   Are you pure slagging me, Whitney?

Whitney   As if, Britney. I'm your biggest fan. Because you buy and sell guys. You put guys through the ringer. You hang guys out to dry. But see, this Jarvis one: he'll no see you like I see you.

Britney   How'll he see me?

Whitney (*aside*)   As an annoying wee cow he wants to slap. (*To* **Britney**.) No, just be like what I tell you to be like with him.

Britney   So what am I to be like with him?

Whitney   Be yourself.

Britney   I canny.

Whitney   How no?

Britney   It's that long since I've been myself I've forgot who I'm are.

Whitney   Well, don't start asking him what kind of car he's got. Don't push your tits out or shoogle your snatch. And don't – for fuck's sake – start asking him the size of his knob. Seemingly, he's not got much of a one. But don't let that put you off, Britney. Because he is an assistant manager at Best Burgers. So he'll likely buy you a bungalow in the suburbs with two hundred TV channels, a jacuzzi and a totally excellent brand new CD player.

Britney   Will he buy me a pile of CDs as well?

Whitney   Thought you didny need any.

Britney   What are you talking about? There's hunners of CDs I want.

Whitney   Like what?

Britney   Something with love in the title or something.

Whitney   These record shops are dead smart, in't they? Add love to the titles ay CDs just to pull in the punters.

Britney   What's a punter, Whitney? Is it like a cunt?

Whitney   Aye, Britney. Because that's exactly what these record shops have made ay ye: a right cunt! An' good oan them!

Britney (*confused*)   Gonny you stop talking shite, Whitney. And totally get this soft knobhead in here to me!

Jarvis (*off*)   What the fuck is this place?

Whitney   That's him coming now.

Britney   Oh, fuck, no. Pure isny, is it?

Whitney   Why? What's wrong, Britney?

Britney   I'm just urny ready to be myself yet.

Britney *goes off one way,* **Whitney** *chasing after her as* **Jarvis** *and* **Ringo** *come on another way.* **Jarvis** *is dressed as an ecowarrior, he's carrying a large placard with 'Cunthill Ecowarriors' on it and he's holding a half-eaten burger and an open can of juice.*

Jarvis   Costly Coffee shop in the middle of nowhere?

Ringo   Isny a Costly Coffee shop.

Jarvis   Corporate capitalist colonising bastards! Not only have youse taken o'er the whole entire St Eunuch Centre and the whole entire length of Suckingcock Street, now youse're even taking o'er the middle of nowhere as well.

He finds **Celine***'s uniform, picks it up and spits on it before dumping it again.*

Fucking capitalist tat! So what is it if it isny a Costly Coffee shop?

Ringo (*proud*)   The Costly Coffee Scottish regional training centre!

Jarvis   So what's my Celine doing in a training centre?

Ringo   To get trained as a manager. What do you think?

Jarvis   Talking shite, wee man. No way would she do that to me! I totally told my Celine about Costly getting their coffee at knock-down prices from impoverished third-world countries. I totally told her about Costly's serious infringements of staff rights and miscellaneous anti-union practices. I totally told her about Costly's aggressive monopolisation of prime high-street locations and their undercutting of small independent businesses. I only let her take the Costly job to fend off starvation and to let her make a contribution to the Ecowarriors of Cunthill. So where the fuck is she?

Ringo   She'll be here in a minute.

Jarvis   And who are you?

Ringo   I'm Ringo, your staff.

Jarvis   What are you talking about?

Ringo   I'm your staff, I'm telling you.

Jarvis   I'm logo-naked, ecofriendly, fully downsized and serially monogamous. What would I want staff for? Now, where's my Celine till I get my tongue touring all around her titanic tits and shimmied all the way up her salivating snatch. Aye, and where is she till she gets my arse rimmed and my cock sucked? I like a woman that's tongue's evolved with years of practice into a perfect fit for both my cuddly wee cock and my aromatic arsehole. Because regular rimming and frequent sucking is statistically proven to be an important force in the creation of a socially cohesive and stable community. So what is she here for?

Ringo   For to get trained.

Jarvis   No, Jim. You're no getting me. Totally read my lips. What's she here for?

Ringo   For to get trained, I'm telling you.

Jarvis   Right, Ringo. You get one more chance to/

Jarvis *is about to smack* **Ringo**.

Ringo   Ronan invited her.

Jarvis   Who the fuck's Ronan?

Ringo   Marlon O'Donnell's boy!

Jarvis   Might have fuckin known. Not content with trying to make every coffee served across the whole entire globe a Costly one. They're also wanting to shag every other cunt's slag. And I'll tell you right now: this Ronan's got no chance with my Celine. My Celine an' me love each another so much it's freaky.

Ringo   So how's love gonny buy Celine's personal trainer, her life manager, her biannual liposuction and all her designer-label weans' togs?

Jarvis   What would Celine want all that shit for? Celine wouldny be Celine if she did. An' this Ronan one's got to learn that women are not a commodity for to buy and sell. And if he hasn't learnt it, my Celine will soon tell him. And if she hasny already told him, I'll tell her to tell him.

Ringo   You canny start upending the honourable traditions ay this nation! Who dae ye think ye are?

Jarvis   What tradition's that?

Ringo   That rich bastards and top totty go together like hard-on and gaping fanny. So you're gonny loss her whatever you do. You should just give in, son. Keep a bit of pride. The totty that's for you will no go by you. Then again, if you dumped Celine and she got off with Ronan, Ronan'd be totally like that: let you stay on in his gorgeous big mansion here for a menagerie à trois.

Jarvis   What's a menagerie à trois?

Ringo   You sleep in one room and Celine and Ronan sleep in another one. Obviously, Ronan'd have to get something out the arrangement for letting you be his pal and making you rich.

Jarvis   Oh no. No way. Totally break my heart to have to listen at their door for shagging noises. I'd have to be forever shooting back to my room for wanks! And what do I want to be rich for?

Ringo   Own set of wheels he'd get you.

Jarvis (*pointing to his legs*)   What's wrong with these wheels here?

Ringo   Own loft apartment in town.

Jarvis   I'll manage with my wee basement, thanks.

Ringo   Hunners of staff running after you.

Jarvis   What do I want staff for?

Ringo   How no?

Jarvis   Because my principles would mean I'd have to have a no-discrimination policy on the grounds of gender, sex, race, age or disability.

Ringo   Nothing to stop you.

Jarvis   Aw, get to fuck. How would you like your house totally stowed out with one-legged geriatric Paki dykes?

Ringo   What about your own personal chef well?

Jarvis   I'm going on a diet.

Ringo   Think of all they gorgeous lovely Best Burgers.

Jarvis   Stop it.

Ringo   All they mouthwatering pizzas.

Jarvis   Aw, this isny fair.

Ringo   An' when it came tae your Orgasmic Fried Chicken it wouldny be so much go large as go giant.

Jarvis   Hardly my fault if I developed a serious junk-food addiction prior to the development ay ma principles, is it?

Britney *comes in.*

Jarvis   Who's the slag?

Ringo   Aw, it's Britney! How's it going, wee doll? (*Aside to* **Jarvis**.) Gorgeous, isn't she?

Jarvis (*aside*)   That's a matter of opinion.

Ringo   C'mere an' I'll gie you an intro.

Jarvis   Aye, you're all right, mate.

Ringo   This is Jarvis, Britney. Jarvis, this is Britney.

Jarvis   I said I'm all right. Is there something wrong wi' you?

Ringo (*finally losing it*)   It's you there's something wrong with. Wee knock-out of a slag standing there. What are you, a poof?

Ringo *goes.*

Jarvis (*aside*)   He's just calling me a poof so I'll pull that wee tart.

Britney (*sweet*)   You go out with Celine McAnespie, don't you?

Jarvis (*cold*)   I do.

Britney   I've heard she's excellent.

Jarvis   (*cold*)   She is.

Britney   Everybody's after her.

Jarvis   Aye, I wish they'd all fuck off and die.

Britney   You can't blame them. She is totally gorgeous. She could be in a girl band and be absolutely massive.

Jarvis   They're wasting their time.

Britney   What does she see in you? Have you got money?

Jarvis   No.

Britney   What drugs do you do?

Jarvis   I don't do drugs.

Britney   Have you got a big cock?

Jarvis   . . . Average. Now could you fuck off?

Britney   Don't tell me to fuck off. I'm only trying to help you.

Jarvis   How can you help me?

Britney   I'm trying to help you understand you've got to back off and let Ronan O'Donnell get fired into Celine.

Jarvis   How do you work that out?

Britney   Because he's better than you. Well, he is. His old man's pure heart attack material so he's going to die ane day and leave all his cars and houses and staff and more staff and Ronan's also got a big cock and he goes to the gym and he's tried every drug there is. So why are you being so selfish and letting Celine knock Ronan back in favour of you and you're a pot-ugly fat bastard?

Jarvis (*hurt*)   It's not my fault I'm ugly.

Britney   You're not ugly.

Jarvis   What did you say I was ugly for then?

Britney   Because I've got a really great personality. I have. People tell me I have. And it's because I've got a really great personality and I'm really, really good-looking I can say the first thing that comes into my head and get away with it.

Jarvis   You shouldny be telling people they're ugly.

Britney   I told you you're not ugly. You're actually quite manly.

Jarvis (*flattered*)   What makes you say that?

Britney   Well, Ronan's got quite a surprising cock seemingly but you're more like a man man. You're the kind of guy a slag wants to ram her up against a wall and fuck her stupid.

Jarvis   What?

Britney (*irritated*)   What what?

Jarvis   What's it to you if I'm manly?

Britney   Why do you want to know?

Jarvis   Why shouldn't I?

Britney   Why should you?

Jarvis (*aside*) Here we go. (*To* **Britney**.) Bit of a flirt, you!

Britney   You can't say that.

Jarvis   Aye, I can. An' look at the state ay you. A' this shite just to get people to like you.

Britney   What's wrong wi' getting people tae like you?

Jarvis   It's against my principles getting people to like you. And it husny worked. I still don't like you. Now fuck off.

Britney   You totally canny talk to me like that.

Jarvis   How no?

Britney   Because I'm going to be a supermodel when I grow up.

Jarvis   You'll be a slut when you grow up.

Britney   That is so uncool talking to an innocent young girl like that.

Jarvis   I'm not wrong to call you a slut. You're wrong to be one. Hardly know me and you're all over me.

Britney   How am I?

Jarvis   Your breasts are sticking out, your arse is sticking out, and your tongue's hanging out. An' my women don't come on to me. I come on to them.

Britney   Your arse is totally out the window, ya bam.

Jarvis   Every word you say's reducing your chances of getting off with me. Not that you ever had any.

Britney   Are you like stoned or what? No way am I into you. I've seen better dugs.

Jarvis   OK, you want to get into my pants, right?

Britney   Do I fuck!

Jarvis   You've got no chance. Because, see, if I told you about my Celine: you'd be gutted. Because, see, when I met her: she said nothing, she knew nothing, she shagged nobody. But I saw the potential in Celine. So I gave her her confidence. I gave her her politics. Then I gave her my knob. Whereas with you: I wouldny give you the shite out my arse. Now get to fuck. Celine's coming.

He waves **Britney** *out.*

Britney   Fuck off yourself, knobhead.

He pushes her out.

Get your hands off me, you/ you lovely big hunky man, you.

She grabs on to him as **Ringo** *comes in.*

Jarvis (*separating*)   Wee slag's been totally trying to kiss my knob.

Britney   No way would I kiss your cheesy wee knob. That's disgusting. Mean, if your knob was a half-decent size I'd just wipe yer cheese off first, then kiss it.

Jarvis   Where's Celine?

Ringo (*to* **Jarvis**)   Waitin' on ye. 'Mon, we'll catch up with her.

Jarvis *and* **Ringo** *go off as* **Ronan** *and* **Whitney** *come on.*

Whitney (*to* **Britney**)   Right, Britney: you hooked in Jarvis yet?

Britney   Don't talk to me about him.

Whitney   He never blanked you?

Britney *appears upset.*

Whitney   What is it, wee doll? You can tell your big sister Whitney.

Britney (*hurt*)   He said I'm a total slag.

Whitney   You *are* a total slag.

Britney   Aye, but nobody's ever told me I'm a total slag before. I usually tell them I'm one.

Whitney   At least you know now what people think of you.

Britney   I don't know if I want to know. I'm gonny kill myself. I'm depressed.

Whitney   Aw, my wee doll. Tell you what. If you really want to kill yourself, your big sister Whitney will give you a hand.

Ronan   I ah/ I ah/

Whitney   Breathe, Ronan.

Ronan   What . . . are . . . we . . . going . . . to . . . do . . . now?

Whitney   You leave it to Whitney.

Ronan   Can . . . we . . . not . . . throw . . . him . . . out?

Whitney   Aye, and Celine will march straight after him!

Ronan   So what . . . exactly . . . are . . . you . . . planning?

Whitney   I don't plan it. I do it. I just do it. (*Aside.*) Well I do! See, I'm the kind of slag that sails through her period. Aerobics. Mountaineering. I can even go to a Tupperware party and feel no fear. Swoosh. Just . . . do . . . it. Swoosh. Just . . . do . . . it. Ha ha. (*To* **Ronan** *and* **Britney**.) Upstairs, youse two.

Ronan *goes up to the office.* **Britney** *goes to go and comes back.*

Britney   I'm no going up there with him. He gives me the creeps. He's too stuttery.

Whitney   Come with me well, pest.

Whitney *goes to go. She spots* **Celine***'s uniform, picks it up and hides it behind counter. Then she charges out, followed by* **Britney** *as* **Jarvis** *comes on in a rage, followed by* **Ringo**.

Jarvis   Celine's no back here either, cuntface. So where is she?

Ringo   She went off looking for you, I'm telling you.

Jarvis *belts* **Ringo**.

Ringo   Oh fuck. Oh shite. I canny believe you did that. What about your principles?

Jarvis *belts* **Ringo** *again*.

Ringo   Oh, ya cunt, ya cunt, ya cunt. Gonny no hit us again. You're too good to start kicking fuck out of people. Whereas I'm all the dross and shite of the/

Jarvis   Make me sick, you guys. Colluding in your own oppression at the hands of all the capitalist monopolising bastards! So fuck off, dross, uh? Fuck off, shite.

Jarvis *goes to hit* **Ringo** *again*. **Ringo** *goes to run away but runs into something, hurts himself and falls over.*

Ringo   Oh. Oh. Oh. Oh. Could you not get hold of a few non-violent principles?

Jarvis   I'm stowed out with the bastards! But my taking action against the forces of oppression principles got the better of my non-violent principles on this occasion.

Ringo   It's the O'Donnells you should be battering fuck out of. I only work here.

Jarvis   You shouldn't be working here.

Ringo   I've got to work for someone.

Jarvis   You should be working to save the planet.

Ringo   I'm working to pay off my credit card.

Jarvis   You shouldn't have a credit card. So see you: you're compromised, so you are. And all compromise is death.

Ringo   And dead's what you'll be if you don't head. I'm going. I'm going.

Ringo *goes off as* **Whitney** *comes on with* **Celine** *who is now wearing ecowarrior clothes.*

Celine (*coming in running*)   Aw, Jarvis, Jarvis, Jarvis. Look at you. Gonny get your merchandise out and I'll suck you till you come! In fact: c'mere. C'mere darling. Because you're the best merchandise in the whole entire mall, so you are. And see me: I'm as high as all they daft slags that run about like loonies in the fanny pad adverts!

Jarvis   Aw, you couldny be as high as me. I'm as high as an ecowarrior helicopter attacking the multinational businesses engaged in the extraction of non-renewable fossil fuels from ecologically sensitive environments.

Celine   You couldny be as high as me. I'm as high as a Cheapsave plastic bag stuck up on a Novaphone mast on the top of a multi-storey.

Jarvis   You couldny be as high as me. I'm as high as the hole in the ozone layer.

Celine   And you couldn't be as high as me. Because I'm so in love with you it's freaky!

Jarvis   I'm so in love with you it's freaky!

They kiss.

Whitney   Right, fair enough. Youse're totally freaked out in love with each another. But gonny no go on about it. My eyes are filling up. I'll be pure bealing if my mascara runs, Celine.

Celine   Do you still wear mascara?

Whitney   I do. Is that bad?

Celine   Well, it's against the principles my Jarvis taught me! Oh, and this here's Jarvis.

Whitney   Pleased to meet you, Jarvis. (*Aside.*) Oh my fuck, by the way. I didny expect Jarvis to be so hunky! I'll totally need to try and make it look no too obvious.

Jarvis   How are you doing, Whitney? (*To* **Celine**.) You still into me, Celine?

Celine   Totally, big man. You?

Jarvis   Totally. Mean: look at you. You're standing there like a Best Burgers Double Cheeseburger. With extra bacon.

Whitney   Great to see such a happy loving couple, so it is. Youse put me in mind of me and an old shag of mine. Nine inches. Went all night. Died though. On the job. Shot his load and a cardiac arrest at the exact same moment. But I'll say this for him: even after he died he kept his hard-on for another couple of hours. I did the right thing by him though. Didny try and bring him off or anything. Regret it now though. Be a smashing wee story to tell your grandchildren. 'It's totally true, kids, your old gran brung off a corpse.' And before we go any further, those cunts at Costly Coffee have totally made a rule that it's Costly Coffee-only personnel in the training centre. But don't you guys worry. Marlon's away to London for the weekend and I, for one, willny tell a soul. So, Jarvis, you stay on as long as you want, pal. You're very welcome.

Celine   Aw, thanks, Whitney.

Jarvis   That's awfy good of you, Whitney. But we'll probably just get up the road.

Whitney   Whatever youse want. Nice to meet youse both. I'll go and get Brad and we'll can start the course.

Celine   We're no going up the road, Jarvis. The wumman's totally offering us her hospitality.

Jarvis   Aye, but this is Costly Coffee, Celine.

Celine   Aye, but it's Whitney no Costly that's invited us. And what about Brad? I need to say goodbye to him first. Totally lovely guy. An' you'll have to meet him.

Whitney *goes out.*

Celine   So how come you gave me a beamer for in front of Whitney?

Jarvis   Shouldny be taking beamers in front of the likes of Whitney!

Celine   How no?

Jarvis   Because she's an assimilated monopolising capitalist bastard!

Celine   Aye, but as assimilated monopolising capitalist bastards go, she's fuckofa nice!

Jarvis   I'll gie you that, Celine. Do you reckon she might be fighting capitalism from inside the system?

Celine   Bet you that's exactly what she's doing! (*Cheerfully.*) I thought there was something no right about her!

Jarvis   I really missed you, Celine.

Celine   And I missed you, Jarvis.

Jarvis   So have you let Ronan shag you yet?

Celine   Aw, you know I wouldny let anyone else shag me. Mean, I was totally scared because I didny shag you this morning you'd think I'd went off you and dump me.

Jarvis   Och, Celine, doll. Not even the entire assembled might of the Costly Coffee Company could make me dump you.

Celine   Aye, but I'm scared it will.

Jarvis   You've nothing to be scared ay, Celine. We're strong, you an' me. We're principled. An' we're the Ecowarriors of Cunthill.

Celine   Aye, but I'm are still scared.

Jarvis *bursts into tears.*

Celine   What is it?

Jarvis   It's you being scared. I canny stand it. Gonny no be!

Celine   I'm urny scared.

Jarvis   Aye, you are!

Celine   Aye, but from now on I'll no be. So gonny always love me, uh?

Jarvis   I'll love you, Celine, till all the sewers run dry.

Celine   I'll love you, Jarvis, till all the condoms burst.

Jarvis   Us two are going to get happiness injected into us. So it canny get back out.

Celine (*aside*)   He's like: 'Injected.' Where does he get all those words? They just keep coming out of him. Hunners and hunners of words. He's like a big . . . fat . . . bastard. Bastard? What did I say that for? I didn't mean he was a fat bastard. I meant he was a fat fountain of words. A fat fountain of words. That's what I meant. (*To* **Jarvis**.) But how come your protest wis called off?

Jarvis   Because Costly Coffee's just shut down their Monknock village HQ and flitted to London. They're stabbin' their exploited Scottish work-force in the back an' giein' up hunners ay millions ay grants off the Scottish government just tae get the prestige ay havin' their HQ in an international capital.

Celine   But Costly don't exploit *all* their workers, Jarvis.

Jarvis   What are you talking about, Celine? Course they do.

Celine   The shop managers get six pounds an hour.

Jarvis   You're no thinking about becoming a Costly Coffee shop manager, are you?

Celine   How no?

Jarvis   That's a capitalist action. Playing the job market. You'd get assimilated!

Celine   Well, you're always saying we're all capitalists nowadays because it's a capitalist world we're living in.

Jarvis   Aye, but we're meant to be fighting capitalism. No joining in with it.

Celine   Aye, but could we no fight capitalism fae inside the system wi' Whitney? Mean, out of my three pound an hour I gie 50p to the Ecowarriors of Cunthill. Just think, if I became a Costly Coffee manager I could increase it to 75p or even a/

Whitney *and* **Ringo** *come on.*

Ringo   That's your ma on the phone for you, Celine.

Celine   My ma? My lovely wee ma? How did she know I was here?

Ringo   I phoned her and told her.

Celine   How did you get her number?

Ringo   Out your bag, Celine.

Celine   That was awful good of you, Ringo. Because I totally love that wee wumman! I totally love her! I totally love her!

Celine *follows* **Ringo** *out.*

Whitney   You not better go with her?

Jarvis   Aye, you're all right. She likes to talk about me not to me when she's talking to her mother. Can I no just wait here with you?

Whitney   Maybe we shouldny. Just the two of us. No here. Know what I mean?

Jarvis   What *do* you mean?

Whitney   Fulla gossips, this place. Never know when someone's watching you.

Ronan *is looking through the office window.*

Jarvis   So is it right you're fighting capitalism fae the inside?

Whitney (*confidentially*)   How did you know?

Jarvis   You can always tell the good guys from the wanks!

Ringo *comes on.*

Ringo   That's the lunch getting served.

Whitney   Is it that time already? We'll just have to put the training off till the afternoon. Just come through now if you like.

Jarvis   You inviting me for lunch?

Whitney (*aside*)   I'll gie Jarvis lunch any time he wants! (*To* **Jarvis**.) Of course I am, Jarvis.

Jarvis   Might as well, I suppose. Celine will be hours. You know what you slags are like.

Whitney   What are we like?

Jarvis   Youse can go at it for hours.

Whitney   At what for hours?

Jarvis   You know. With your yakking.

Jarvis *rushes out.* **Whitney** *and* **Ringo** *share a look, thumbs up and follow him.* **Ronan** *remains looking out.*

Act Two

Ronan is still looking out from the office when **Whitney** *and* **Celine** *come on together.* **Celine** *is dressed in very revealing clothes. She is carrying plastic bags with Greatgirl, Cute Clothing and CNUT labels.* **Whitney** *clocks that* **Ronan** *is still there and signals him to wait.*

Celine   So I'm just off the phone to my ma, Whitney. These wee slags come up. They're like: 'Come with us. Come with us.' Course I'm totally expecting to get took into my lunch. Next thing I know I'm in a big fuck-off room one hundred per cent stowed with brand new claes. They're like: 'Try this on, Celine. Try that on.' I'm here to get trained to be a manager no to get fobbed off with new outfits. An' next thing ye know my ain claes is in the bin!

Whitney   Did ye no take them back oot?

Celine   No I did not. The bin's full ay Costly shite and spunk. So I'm urny putting up with it. Now where's that Brad one?

Whitney   Neither you should. Total neck on them, so they have. Front.

Celine   And I look a total and utter tube as well. Jarvis will kill me. And it isny as though it's even me.

Whitney   Oh, but it is you. You do look gorgeous.

Celine   Maybe just keep this one well. But no more! And that wasny all. I mean: next thing the wee lassies are like: 'We heard you're shagging that hunky Ronan. Is he a good ride? Does he talk dirty to you? What size is his knob?' I'm like: 'Gonny you wee slags fuck off and leave me alone.' Wonder where Brad is!

Whitney   You just gie me their names, Celine. I'll get them a' sacked!

Celine   Aye, you're all right, Whitney! Because finally the
wee slags fuck off. I'm like that: 'How'm I gonny get back to
Jarvis?' Then this guy comes up. The one you found me
with. He's like: 'I'll take you.' Aye, take me the long way
round, he means. And all the time he's like: 'Did you hear
the one about this? Did you hear the one about that?'
Wouldny of minded, Whitney, but half his jokes are about
poofs, Pakis and poor people! So I totally hate it here,
Whitney. Mean: every single one of them's like that: dump
Jarvis, get off with Ronan. I tried to tell them about trust. I
tried to tell them about commitment. I tried to tell them
about loving someone so fuckin much you'd suck them off in
the middle of the St Eunuch Centre. But oh no. It's me
that's to get a life. I'm heading as soon as Jarvis gets back.
But where is Brad? Wouldny like to leave and no say
cheerio to the guy. Him being so nice. Mean: imagine him
coming all the way from Yankeeland to get trained to be a
manager! What a guy, uh? So how can you stand it here,
Whitney?

Whitney   Too much, aren't they? They're all telt to make
Ronan happy. Fuck everyone else. Don't bother with them,
Celine. You just stick in with your pal, Whitney.

Celine   You are so ace, by the way. But where's this
Brad? Brad! What do I keep goin' on about Brad for? I
mean: where's Jarvis?

Whitney   Still at his lunch.

Celine   Oh, stupid question.

Whitney   You're no thinking of trading Jarvis in, Celine?

Celine   No I'm are not. But, see, if I was, I totally
wouldn't be looking for anything special. None of your filthy
rich Ronans. Something hunky but ordinary would do me.
Someone like that Brad guy.

Whitney   Will I call him for you?

Celine   Don't you dare, Whitney! I don't want to see him. Well, I do. Well, I don't. Not yet. I mean: look at the state of me.

Whitney   Gonny just stop running yourself down, Celine. Brad will likely take one look at you and totally get a big fat hard-on. Ronan too, by the way.

Celine   In that case, I'm definitely getting changed! My uniform'll do the now. Where'd I put it?

Celine *has a look for it.* **Britney** *appears.* **Whitney** *waves her away.* **Britney** *stays at the back out of sight to* **Celine**.

Whitney   Ronan's no as bad as he's made out to be, Celine. He's actually the shy type when you get to know him.

Celine *stops looking.*

Celine   Well, I must admit all the wee slags that work in here are all like that: pure dump all their guys to go out with Ronan. I must be a weirdo. Totally liking my big fat ugly boring slob of a Jarvis. We're well matched, I suppose. I'm aye the dorky one hanging back hiding like the music in the background. Whereas they're all sticking their tits out at anything the least wee bit hunky. But at least they know how to make something of theirselves. Whereas with me what you see is what you get: shite!

Whitney   Ronan's totally gagging for slags that speak their minds, Celine. Took a lot of bullshit in his life, the boy, in this place! Sure you don't want me to call him in for you?

Celine   Aw naw! You canny. If Ronan came up to me, instead of nutting the cunt I'd more than likely be like that: all tongue-tied and pure beamer, Whitney.

Whitney   But no comparison between you an' the wee slags that work in here: OK, they're nice enough to your face, but see behind your back . . . ?

Celine   What have the slags been saying about me?

Whitney   'Pot ugly. Dresses totally untrendy. Personality totally no bubbly. BO on her totally monging.' 'Dug her, bitch, no tits lesbo.'

Celine (*angry*)   Aye, but how come Ronan wants to totally go out with me and pure hates their guts if I'm the dug?

Whitney *signals* **Ronan** *to come down.*

Whitney   They all think Ronan's crazy about you because you're different fae them. And he'll go off you when he gets to know you.

Celine   I'd totally get off with Ronan just to spite they wee slags.

Ronan *reaches the bottom of the stairs.*

Whitney   I'd totally love that, Celine. I'd/

Celine   Oh my fuck, it's Brad. How come they Yanks are all so hunky? Do I look all right? No, don't answer that. Don't care how I look. But do I look *no too* bad?

While **Celine** *is distracted with* **Ronan,** **Whitney** *signals* **Britney** *to come in.*

Britney *stares at* **Celine** *very obviously and gives her a girly wave. She looks snubbed when* **Celine** *doesn't return the wave.*

Ronan   Hey.

Celine (*aside*)   He's so cute the way he says 'hey'. (*To* **Ronan**.) Hey Brad!

Ronan   Wowee, Celine. You look so amazing.

Celine   Do I? Oh fuck, do I? So do you. (*Aside.*) Oh shite. I canny believe I said that. What if he gets the wrong idea? (*To* **Ronan**.) Thanks very much, Brad.

Ronan   You're welcome, Celine.

Celine (*putting* **Ronan** *off*)   And Jarvis will be in in a minute, so he will. I'll introduce yeez when he finally stops stuffing his fat face. I/ (*Aside.*) Oh Jesus Christ, what's wrong with me, slagging my Jarvis like that? Brad'll totally get the wrong idea now. (*To* **Ronan**.) I didny mean/

Britney *changes position to be seen better by* **Celine** *and does another girly wave.* **Celine** *does her best to ignore* **Britney**.

Celine (*aside*)   What's that cow waving at me for? Probably more slagging. That's all I get in this place. I'm definitely gonny ignore her. (*To* **Ronan**.) And Jarvis says he's/

Britney *comes forward in a rage.*

Britney (*to* **Celine**)   How come you're like that: totally blanking me?

Celine (*improvising*)   Because/ Because waving's totally tacky. It's cheesy. It's for posers. It isny real.

Britney   How come waving's tacky? Is saying goodbye at the airport tacky? Is the queen tacky? Is people drowning tacky? (*Theatrically to others.*) What is she like?

Celine (*taking the piss*)   I don't know. What am I like, slag?

Whitney   You tell her, Celine.

Ronan   You're way out of order, miss. You should apologise to Celine.

Britney (*to* **Ronan**)   Get to fuck. It's her. I was only trying to be nice and/ Because everybody's raving about you. Seemingly you've got everybody pishing theirselves laughing at you! So say something funny gonny, uh?

Celine   I doubt it, by the way. My jokes go down like used condoms.

Britney (*laughing*):   Well weird, isn't she? Modesty's like totally uncool, Celine. Did you no know that?

Celine   That's it. She heads or I head.

Ronan   You heard what Celine said. You're out of here.

Britney   Youse can't make me go.

Whitney Get out. Come on. I've got a training to get on with.

Britney I can't get out of here quick enough, by the way. (*To* **Ronan**.) You coming? Come on. I'll let you shag me.

Ronan Thank you for your offer, Britney. I'm flattered at your interest. Unfortunately, I don't share it.

Britney Your loss, twat! And see if you end up getting off with Celine? Guarantee you'll be going out with her an hour and you'll totally want to top yourself.

Britney *goes out.*

Celine This place is getting worse. Accosted, insulted and the pish ripped out me by a slag. And a' in one day! It's like her standards are in the gutter and I'm urny up to them! Hope not, by the way. Do my nut in to be like her!

Whitney Don't you let her get to you, Celine! Mean, when trash like that starts ripping the pish out of you at least you know you're doing *something* right.

Ronan (*to* **Whitney**) Do you have a system available for submitting unfavourable reports? Because you know: Costly Coffee's remarkable reputation could be on the line with stuff like this.

Celine Oh no. She might be trash, but I'm not gonny be the one that got Britney sacked!

Whitney Well, I wouldny want to go against your wishes, Celine. I like you too much.

Celine And you know I like you, Whitney. Great, isn't she, Brad?

Ronan Sure is, Celine! But would you have any objections if I made a personal statement to you?

Celine (*aside*) Oh my fuck! What's he gonny say to me? (*To* **Ronan**.) Sure thing, Brad. Fire away.

Ronan I want to apologise.

Celine   Oh, Brad! What for?

Ronan   Well, I've been waiting around for you.

Celine   So? I've been waiting for you too. All my life as it happens. (*Aside.*) What the fuck did I say that for? (*To* **Ronan**.) Just joking. Ha ha.

Ronan   My intentions towards you were not exclusively honourable.

Celine   What are you trying to say to me?

Ronan   I've been, uh, hoping to take part in some non-verbal communication with you.

Celine   What's that exactly?

Ronan   Is flirting ever practised in Scotland?

Celine   No very often. So gonny no flirt. I willny be able to cope. And I canny exactly flirt back with you!

Whitney   Heh: if you guys want to flirt, go ahead and flirt. It's no as if I'm gonny tell on youse.

Ronan *flirts with* **Celine**.

Celine   Gonny no look at me like that.

Ronan   Like what?

Celine   All hunky and a big ride and I want to shag you senseless. (*Aside.*) I can't believe I just said that. I'm gonny take a pure beamer. (*To* **Ronan**.) I mean flirt wi' ye. Well, I would flirt wi'ye. But I canny. But see if I *did* flirt wi' ye it wid be for one reason and one reason only: to see that slag Britney's sick wee face. But I'm totally trying to do the decent thing and no want to make her sick. So gonny cool it, uh?

Ronan   Well, should your, uh, personal circumstances in any way alter/

Celine (*aside*)   I can just hear my wee ma now. She'd be like: 'Ride him, Celine. He's a smoothie. You'll no get another chance to shag one ay them.' (*To* **Ronan**.) Tell you what, Brad.

Ronan   Uh-huh?

Celine   I'll think about it!

Ronan   Cool!

Whitney   Right that's enough flirting for one day! Youse're flirting away Costly Coffee's valuable time. (*To* **Ronan**.) Could you write one of they reports you mentioned, Brad? Say Britney's shat all over Costly's reputation.

Ronan   Sure thing!

Ronan *goes out.*

Celine   I can't believe this. That guy Brad pure likes me wearing the claes Jarvis hates me wearing!

Whitney   You huvny went and got the hots for Brad, have you?

Celine   Course I huvny. Well, I have. But no as much as I've got them for Jarvis. Mean: at least Jarvis has got principles!

Whitney   Brad's got principles too.

Celine   Has he? What are they?

Whitney   You should ask him yourself.

Celine   Maybe I just will. Aye, maybe I/

Jarvis (*off*)   Where are you, Celine?

Celine   Oh my fuck. I canny let Jarvis see me dressed like an assimilated capitalist slag!

Whitney   Well, go and get your own claes back out the bin, take them to the laundry. Get the wumman to wash them through by hand, stick them in the dryer, be ready for you in no time.

Celine   Aw, Whitney. I love you so much it's freaky.

Celine *rushes out.*

Whitney   I love you so much it's/

Whitney *takes out her mobile.*

We're on our way, Ronan boy. She's biting. She's totally/
. . . What? . . . Och, gonny breathe and stop stuttering . . .
Aye aye aye. Add a few principles to your repertoire and
she'll be knobbing you by midnight.

Jarvis *and* **Ringo** *come on.* **Whitney** *puts her mobile away.*

Whitney   Hey, big man.

Jarvis   Well, come on to fuck, Whitney: youse're sitting
there in the dining room shovelling Best Burgers into your
gob and all around they're like that: knobs going into
mouths, knobs going into arses, knobs going into fannies.
And right next to me, at the actual dining-room table, this
guy's got his hand right up the frock of the woman sitting
next to him. I'm like that: 'Give it a rest, prick. People are
eating their dinner.' He's like that: 'What do you mean, big
man? I'm only slipping her the sweetie.' I'm like that: 'Do
sweeties not normally go in the mouth?' He's like that:
'We'll get on to that in a minute.' So at that point does the
prick not turn round and start laughing hand still up the
slag's frock. Then the slag starts laughing. Then the whole
entire lot of them starts laughing. Even I start laughing.
Sitting there with a honking big hard-on myself, so I was.
Which is well out of order, Whitney. Because how the fuck
can we be expected to create a socially cohesive society with
all that indiscriminate shagging going on?

Whitney (*aside*)   Oh my fuck. A great big stonking hard-on
nestling in under a' they mounds o' fat and I canny even get
my hands on it. I'll ask him if I can bring him off later. Gie
his hard-on time to build up a heid o' steam. (*To* **Jarvis**.)
Och, hand up the frock's an old O'Donnell family tradition,
Jarvis.

Jarvis   Aye, a monopolising colonising capitalist tradition!

Whitney   Loads of them's tried to get it stopped. The tradition's always won oot so faur. But it isny as bad as it seems. Because the hands might be going up the frocks, but they totally don't mean anything by it.

Jarvis (*wonder*)   So there's no disrespect intended?

Whitney   You wouldny put your hand up someone's frock unless you respected them, would you? . . . How did you like the dinner?

Jarvis   Food like I've never shovelled down my gob in my whole entire puff. And did I take a bevvy or did I take a bevvy? Toasted Celine. Toasted you. Toasted my staff. Toasted Ronan. Even toasted my hard-on. Toasted, toasted, toasted, till I'm like that: well puddled.

Whitney   Glad you enjoyed yourself.

Jarvis   Aye, but I didny! Well, I did. But I shouldny've.

Whitney   How no?

Jarvis   Because it's against my principles to enjoy myself.

Whitney   Have you got principles, Jarvis?

Jarvis   I certainly do, Whitney.

Whitney   Gonny tell us what they are.

Jarvis   Well, globalisation is gobbing a' o'er the planet. They multinationals are trying to run the whole entire show to the detriment o' a' the rest o' us. We're voting in governments that have been selt to us wi' multinational money paying for their adverts. Then the multinationals are telling the governments what to do. Aye, they multinationals are totally taking what's rightfully oors and brandin' it an' sellin' it back to us. So once they multinationals has finally took o'er it'll be rock-bottom wages and sky-high prices an' there'll be fuck all we can do about it.

Whitney   Aye but what should we be doing in place o' globalisation, Jarvis?

Jarvis   It should be *localisation* no *globalisation*. Mean: what are we boating in bananas a' the way fae Barbados when we could be bussing in berries fae up the road in Blairgowrie?

Whitney   Ye mean I willny ever be able to slip a banana into my mooth ever again?

Jarvis   Can you no go without the odd banana?

Whitney (*aside*)   . . . No I canny! (*To* **Jarvis**.) Course I can. (*Confidentially*.) Because you an' me's got the exact same principles!

Jarvis (*excited*)   I totally knew that about you, Whitney. I totally knew.

Ringo   Right, cut it out you two. I'm Celine's staff an' a'. An' if she has to ask me what youse two were gettin' up to thegither I'll be totally obliged to tell her.

Jarvis   We urny up to nothing, prick.

Whitney   Aye, you tell him, Jarvis! See you, Ringo. You're a decrepit slice of knobcheese.

Ringo   What are you talking like you're out the gutter for? You're the training manager. No wonder the carpets are covered in spunk stains. Any more ay that an' I'll submit a report to Ronan about you!

Jarvis   Hey, you staff! Get Whitney a bollocking and I'll pickle your dick for you!

Ringo   Canny talk like that tae me! I'm your staff. An' as your staff it's my duty tae tell you that Celine ay yours hates yer guts!

Jarvis   What are you talking about, prick?

Ringo   She prefers someone else to you.

Jarvis   Who?

Ringo   Not for me to say.

Jarvis   Who?

Ringo   I'm not telling you, I said.

Jarvis (*threatening*)   Tell . . . me . . . who!

Ringo   Her ma. She prefers her wee ma to you!

Jarvis *bursts out laughing, joined by* **Whitney**.

Ringo   Aye, laugh a' yeez want. It willny be that when she's back sooking her ma's tits in place o' your knob.

Jarvis   Get to fuck, knobhead.

Whitney   Aye, get out my sight, Ringo gonny. You're doing my nut in.

Ringo   An' see you, Whitney: you're out on your ear!

Ringo *goes out.*

Jarvis   This place just gets worse! Except you, Whitney. You are one slag that has not been assimilated. Mean: at least wi' you I can/ I can/

Whitney   You can what?

Jarvis   Well, at least I can talk to you about anything, can't I?

Whitney   Anything, Jarvis. And can I talk to you about anything?

Jarvis   Totally, Whitney!

Whitney   So what do you want to talk to me about?

Jarvis   I want to talk to you about/ about/ about/ Nothing you want to talk to me about? I'll no tell anyone either. Well, I'll tell Celine. Because I tell my Celine everything. But I'm gonny stop telling her everything. Because she doesny tell me everything.

Whitney   Oh! I canny believe that about Celine. What does Celine no tell you?

Jarvis   She doesny tell me what she says about me to her mother for a start.

Whitney   That's atrocious! For all you know, Celine could be laughing at you for having a wee knob.

Jarvis   What?

Whitney   And for being a dead boring wank goin' on an' on about your principles.

Jarvis (*shocked*)   Who telt you that?

Whitney   Doesny matter who telt me, does it?

Jarvis   Aye, it matters.

Whitney   She maybe didny mean it.

Jarvis   Who telt you?

Whitney   Celine telt me.

Jarvis   Oh my fuck. No my Celine. That's a pure betrayal of my private/ My private/ Well, it's a betrayal of my private parts!

Whitney   Don't be so hard on Celine, Jarvis. It's no her fault if she needs a big knob to satisfy her. Some slags are like that. But no a' o' us are. I mean, I actually prefer wee knobs. Because, see, guys wi' big knobs, they're aye swaggering around swinging their big knobs about giving it: 'No seen one like that before, doll, have you? Gonny go down on us. I'll no keep you long.' No, a wee knob like yours would suit me fine.

Jarvis   Oh, gonny gie us a break. Because talk like that and/ and/ Well, what it does to me is/ is/ Well, I'm not saying what it does to me because what it does to me just isny right!

Whitney   Aye but I couldny *no* talk like that to you.
Because see you, Jarvis: I've been looking at you. And oh
I've been looking at you and you . . . are . . . a king, by the
way!

Jarvis   What are you talking about kings for?

Whitney   Because a king is what you are.

Jarvis   Aye, but gonny no but. Kings against my anti-
royalist principles!

Whitney   Oh! I haven't pissed you off, have I?

Jarvis   No you have not! Have *I* pissed *you* off?

Whitney   How could you piss me off?

Jarvis   By making you think *you* pissed *me* off!

Whitney   You couldny piss me off. Because see your piss,
Jarvis: it's the piss of a/ The piss of a/ Well, if I canny say
it's the piss ay a king, what can I say it is?

Jarvis (*modestly*)   Well, eh, you could always say it's the piss
ay a Jarvis, Whitney!

Whitney   See you: you've totally got the piss ay a Jarvis,
Jarvis!

Jarvis   Aw, thanks.

Whitney   Only thing I'm pissed off about is Ringo
submitting an unfavourable report about me and me getting
sacked and chucked out the building before I can get your
phone number off you. (*Building to hysterics.*) Because if I
don't see you again, I might as well just top myself! Sorry.

Jarvis   Don't be sorry. Because I was totally intending to
gie you my phone number. You're no getting away fae me
that easily!

Whitney   Aw, see you, Jarvis. You've totally inspired me
to/

Jarvis   Inspired you to what?

Whitney   Och, it doesny matter!

Jarvis   Naw, Whitney. Inspired ye tae what?

Whitney   Inspired me to/ to ask if I can gie you a blow job! I can't believe I said that, Jarvis. I'm gonny take a beamer. (*Aside.*) Aye, as if!

Jarvis (*aside*)   She's obviously one o' they romantics!

Whitney (*aside*)   I've embarrassed him. I've went too far.

Jarvis (*aside*)   But would you look at that big hard-on-sized gob on her! So if Celine willny come off the phone and stop yakking about me to her mother I'll totally *deserve* a blow job.

Whitney (*aside*)   No, I'll definitely need to pull back! And I'm no talking about his foreskin!

Jarvis   Thanks for the offer, Whitney! But I couldny dae that to my Celine. Walking in and seeing yer gob a' o'er my bollocks. Well, I'd at least have to ask her first. But I couldny. Och, my brain's mince.

Whitney (*to* **Jarvis**)   Och, I was just joking, Jarvis. Ha ha ha.

Damon and **Ringo** *appear out of sight of* **Jarvis**. **Whitney** *sees them and waves them out to wait.*

Whitney (*to* **Jarvis**)   I was just joking. Ha ha ha.

Jarvis   Well, I obviously knew you wouldny gie me a blow job? Ha ha ha. I mean: would you?

Whitney   It's you that willny want me to give you one. Because lined up alongside Celine I'm/

Jarvis   Total opposite, by the way. If you and Celine were lined up I'd/

Whitney   Oh, gonny button it, uh? You've got my heid spinning, my tits heaving, and my fanny throbbing. So I'm heading.

Whitney *goes upstairs waving* **Ringo** *and* **Damon** *on and goes into the office.*

Jarvis (*aside*)   Aw no, ma staff again! I'm oot ay here.

Jarvis *looks round to find a way out and nips upstairs, watching from the balcony.*

Ringo   Canny credit yer man no turnin' up, son.

Damon   Must of get raided, da.

Ringo   Well, just you do what yer da telt you. I'll see you all right.

Damon   Cheers, da. Where is the cunt?

Damon *looks up.*

Ringo   No, don't look, ya tube.

Damon *and* **Ringo** *speak more confidingly.* **Jarvis** *gets paranoid.*

Damon   Aw, no him, da. No him. Wank totally rammed into us at the Shag Shack Club one night, da. I'm heading.

Damon *goes to go.*

Ringo   You canny head, son.

Ringo *tries to stop him.*

Jarvis (*snapping*)   Hey, staff. Get your hands off that wee guy.

Damon *and* **Ringo** *stop.*

Jarvis   I'll get you done for sexual harassment.

Damon (*confidentially*)   Is he saying you're a poof, da?

Ringo   Ignore him, son. The cunt's a bam.

Damon   You urny a poof. Mean: the only guy you've ever shagged is me, da.

Ringo   No, I huvny. I'd've remembered if I'd shagged ye, son!

Damon   Aye, you did. You and my old uncle totally gang-banged me when I was two.

Ringo   Well, I couldny exactly shag your mother, could I? Have you seen the state of her?

Jarvis   Hey, staff. I told you to/

Ringo (*to* **Jarvis**)   Guy here wants a word.

Jarvis   Well, I don't. (*Aside.*) I know that cunt, by the way. Total clubber. Saw him at the Shag Shack Club. Stripped down to his arse. Up the podium giving it. (**Jarvis** *gestures 'mindless' drug dancing to audience.*) Same thing night after fuckin' night. No wonder the planet's on its last legs. Full ay wanks like that.

Ringo   Catch youse later!

Ringo *goes and* **Jarvis** *comes down.*

Jarvis (*after* **Ringo**)   Aye, get out my sight. And take the android with you!

Damon   All right there, big man?

Jarvis   Don't all right me. You rammed into us at the Shag Shack Club. An' I totally took it. I'm like: 'How's it going?' You're like: totally turned round and blanked us!

Damon   Aw naw, man. No me! I don't blank guys.

Jarvis   Well, some cunt totally identical to you blanked me!

Damon   Must of been wasted, big man. Must of been totally wasted if I blanked you. You're sound, so you are. You're solid.

Jarvis   Less shite. What dae ye want tae say tae me?

Damon   Couldny put in a good word for us wi' Whitney, could ye?

Jarvis   Get tae fuck.

Damon Gonny big man, eh? Because she's gaggin' fer a knobbin' an' I wouldny mind giein' her ane an' totally movin' in wi' her doon here.

Jarvis Wasting yer time, Jim. No way she'd be interested in you.

Damon Be on the streets, man. Be homeless if I don't move in here wi' Whitney. Mean, back up home it's really bad, my man. It's really bad. Fucking estate there, man. All junkees there, man. All the pushers there, man. All the lenders. An' a' the pervs. An' my junkee pisshead ay a ma. And my dirty old cunt uncle that totally shagged me when I was two. Wouldny of minded, man, but the old cunt never even asked my permission to shag me when I was two! So I've got tae get my shit together an get oot ay there, man.

Jarvis Yer uncle's no *still* shagging you is he?

Damon Aw naw, man.

Jarvis So what's the problem?

Damon I kick fuck out of him, my man. Every time I see him I kick fuck out him. *That's* the problem. And the problem is I'm gonny end up killing him. I kicked fuck out of him on his ninetieth birthday there. Chronic there, man. Bad scene up there the now, man. Bad scene up there! So gonny put in a good word fer us wi' Whitney, uh?

Jarvis Sorry, Jim. Couldny dae that tae the wumman.

Damon Well, gonny put in a good word fer my big fat pal Baz. He's got a wee knob on him as well. An' that's the type Whitney pure goes fer!

Jarvis Who told you that?

Damon A' big hunky guys wi' massive knobs that work here. They've a' totally tried it on wi' her an' she totally gie'd them a' a knock back. So gonny totally put in a good word for my big fat pal to Whitney, uh?

Jarvis What's in it fer you?

Damon   Nuthin', man. I'm totally just helping Whitney, my man. An' ma big fat pal Baz, man.

Jarvis   Tell you what, gonny no help her! If Whitney's wantin' a big fat guy wi a wee knob to get off with, *I'll* get her one.

Damon   Aw excellent, man. Thanks fer daein' that fer Whitney, my man. You're cool as fuck, by the way.

Damon *goes out.*

Jarvis (*to audience*)   Oh, Whitney, Whitney, Whitney doll. Whitney, Whitney, Whitney. What I could dae tae you. What I could/ An' where the fuck's Celine? She canny be still yakking to her wee ma. Aye she can. About me and my fat wobbly arse likely. An' my wee knob that's so wee she canny get any satisfaction oot o' it likely. So if there's a spare bit of A1 fat bastard top male totty wi' a wee knob goin' an' that's what Whitney's looking for an' she's totally fighting capitalism fae the inside, surely to fuck I canny have any principles that'll stop me offering her my big fat hard-on for Whitney to totally bring off? Well, can I?

Celine *appears, back in her ecowarrior clothes, slightly downbeat. When* **Whitney** *sees* **Celine** *come in, she slips out of the office on to the open mezzanine to eavesdrop.*

(*Aside.*)   Aye, I can! Oh fuck me, I can! And it goes by the name o' Celine. Because Celine might be like that: yak yak yak about me to her mother. But at the end of the day she's still my Celine, she knows my wee knob inside out and I love her so much it's freaky!

He looks round at **Celine**. *Then away.*

Celine   . . . So what you been up to?

Jarvis   Nothing. Just waiting for you to come off the phone.

Celine   Didny mind me talking to my ma, Jarvis?

Jarvis   Course no.

Short pause.

Celine   Urny yourself.

Jarvis   Aye I'm are myself! Are you yourself?

Celine (*unconvincingly*)   Aye, I'm myself. You know me. Always get me the same way!

Jarvis   You ready to go then?

Celine   Aye, I'm ready! Are you?

Jarvis   Och aye.

Pause. They don't move.

Celine   Och, gonny stop bugging me, Jarvis.

Jarvis   I'm urny bugging you. How am I bugging you?

Celine   You're saying you're going and you're no even making a move.

Jarvis   Well, neither are you making a move!

Celine   I was waiting for *you* to make a move!

Jarvis   I was waiting for *you*!

Short pause.

Celine   So are you heading or no?

Jarvis (*irritably*)   I'm heading, Celine, OK?

Celine   Aye, but *are* you?

Jarvis   Aye, I'm are. Are you?

Celine   Aye, I'm telling you. No, I'm no. I canny. Well, I need to say cheerio to Whitney first!

Jarvis   Me too, by the way.

Celine   So why didn't you say?

Jarvis   Why didn't you?

Short pause.

Celine   And I need to say cheerio to Brad as well! Is that OK?

Jarvis   Why should it no be?

Short pause.

Celine   See! I knew it! There is something wrong wi' ye!

Jarvis   No there isny.

Celine   Aye there is. So what is it?

Jarvis   Nothing.

Celine   No! What is it?

Jarvis   Right. This is it. I'm just gonny pure ask you!

Celine   Well, ask me well.

Jarvis   I'm gonny. I'm gonny. I/

Celine *clenches her teeth.*

Jarvis   Well, do you or don't you agree wi' my principles?

Celine   What are you asking that for? You know I do.

Jarvis   And do you like my wee knob?

Celine   I love your wee knob. How?

Jarvis   Does it satisfy you?

Celine   Course it does. (*Aggressively.*) Did some cunt say it didny?

Jarvis   No! How?

Celine   Don't how me! It was you that asked! When I think of the sacrifices I've made for your principles!

Jarvis   Like what?

Celine   Like wearing a' this shite for a start!

Jarvis (*gobsmacked*)   But you're dressed in a' the best unbranded low-cost claes made wi' one hundred per cent ecologically sound fully biodegradable materials that money can buy!

Celine   Aye, an' no cunt likes them but!

Jarvis   Who telt you that?

Celine   It doesny matter!

Jarvis   Who telt you?

Celine   Shut the fuck up gonny!

Jarvis   Who telt you?

Celine   Brad telt me! Well, he didny. He pure just telt me I looked excellent in/ in/ in some other claes I was wearing at the time. Well, I wisny wearing them. Well, I wis. I wis pure just trying them on but!

Jarvis   You sure you werny wearing they claes to get people to like you?

Celine   Well, I know getting people to like you's against your principles, but at the end of the day what exactly's wrong wi' getting people to like you?

Jarvis   Because needing to get people to like you's how they capitalist arseholes manipulate a' the fashion victims tae buy their overpriced capitalist crap offa them!

Celine   Mean: if you huvny got any decent claes and you huvny got anybody to like you, what have you got?

Jarvis   You've got your principles, Celine!

Celine   Aye, but I huvny got my principles, Jarvis. I've got your principles!

Short pause.

Jarvis   An' is there anything else you huvny got while we're at it?

Celine   Such as what?

Jarvis   Such as me satisfying you wi' ma wee knob an' giein' you regular orgasms right up your snatch?

Celine   Aw, Jarvis.

Jarvis   What?

Celine   There's no need for smut! You know you satisfy me!

Jarvis   Aye, but do you?

Celine   Aye, I do.

Jarvis (*aside*)   She's lying!

Celine (*aside*)   He knows I'm lying! (*To* **Jarvis**.) Who gives a fuck about orgasms? Orgasms turn me right off, so they do. Aw naw, Jarvis: I love you so much it's freaky and that's a' that matters.

Jarvis (*aside*)   She means it!

Celine (*aside*)   I mean it. Well, I think I mean it. (*To* **Jarvis**.) Do you believe me?

Jarvis   I believe you!

Celine   Well, I'm fuckofa sorry, so I am. Brad's wee bit ay praise's pure went tae my heid so it has. I willny try on any mare claes. An' I promise I'll never break your principles again. Do you forgive me?

Whitney *starts to get alarmed.*

Jarvis   Och, nothing to forgive! So 'mon, doll. We better head before they capitalist swine totally break down wur resistance.

Celine   Do you want to?

Jarvis   Aye, I do. An' no more hanging about saying goodbye to folk. A' this saying hello and goodbye crap! It's one ay the ways a corrupt capitalist globalized society hauds ye in it's clutches an' willny let go! Well you canny get away fae they capitalist bams if they're never here for you to say goodbye to! You coming?

Celine   Aye, a' right. Come on.

They go to go.

Whitney   Aw, there yeez are!

She rushes downstairs.

(*Performing surprise.*) Yeez wirny rushing oot wi'oot saying cheerio, were yeez?

Celine   Course we wirny. We were just goin' off tae look for you.

Jarvis   We wouldny no say goodbye tae you.

Whitney   Thank fuck for which. I'd hate to think wur hospitality was in any way shite!

Celine   Oh, Whitney. It isny shite your hospitality! It's smashing!

Jarvis   Aye, it might be o'errun wi' globalised capitalist swine roon here but the food's great an' you're great an'/

Whitney   Yeez urny just saying that?

Jarvis   Course no.

Whitney   Because regarding the food, they usually do efterninn tea aboot noo, Jarvis.

Jarvis   Would you mind, Celine?

Celine   No! Because what would be the point of me minding?

Jarvis *goes to go.*

Jarvis   Thanks, Whitney doll.

Jarvis *goes one way.* **Britney** *appears another, while* **Celine** *watches* **Jarvis** *go.* **Whitney** *waves* **Britney** *away.*

Celine   Will we go an' say cheerio to Brad now?

Whitney   He'll be in talking tae Ronan. But I'll get him oot for ye.

She goes to take **Celine** *out and stops in her tracks.*

Aw, Celine, I pure promised Ronan you'd let that wee cow Britney apologise to you.

Celine   That was awfy good ay him. But I'm no accepting it. She'll no likely mean it.

Whitney   Aye, she will. Ronan's totally like that to her: she's got tae mean it or she's oot on her ear!

Celine   I'm getting tae like this Ronan.

Whitney   Would you be willing tae meet him now?

Celine   Aye, I'll meet him. As long as he doesny try anything.

Whitney   I'll away and see tae it for ye!

Whitney *goes to go.*

Celine   An' tell Jarvis no to be a' day. And tell him to/ to/ Well, tell him to totally stop worrying about the size of his knob. One and a hauf inches is perfectly adequate.(*Aside.*) Is it fuck. But you don't like to sound greedy. (*To* **Whitney**.) Will you?

Whitney   I will. (*Aside.*) I certainly will.

As **Whitney** *leaves, she waves* **Britney** *in.*

Britney *does her girly wave.*

Britney   Hiya, Celine!

Celine (*aside, ignoring* **Britney**)   Still waving at me after I told her no to.

Britney   What are you blanking me again for? And they all think the sun shines out your arse. Fuck knows why!

Celine   Cut the crap and get on with it, slag!

Britney   On with what?

Celine   Your apology!

Britney   I eh/ I eh/

Celine   For fuck's sake, get on wi' it, gonny!

Britney   Eh . . . ah/

Celine   What are you like? Canny even be nice when you huv tae!

Britney   Well, I'm jealous ay ye!

Celine   How?

Britney   Because Ronan's hunky an' rich and an' he's got a big knob an' he totally prefers you tae me. Which isny right. Mean, I'm gorgeous trendy totty an' it's no my fault if he prefers big ugly slags that build up his confidence!

Celine   Right, that's it. I don't want yer apology now!

Britney   Aye, but, Celine, you've got to tell him he's wasting his time wi' you.

Celine   How do you work that out?

Britney   Well, you've been slagging him off!

Celine   He stared at me through a window. Course I slag him off!

Britney   Aye, but I'd love him to stare at me through a window! So that's a waste ay his time staring at a slag that doesny like it. So could you no totally slag him off to his face and tell him to shag me instead!

Celine   I've stopped slagging him.

Britney   You into him now?

Celine   I didny say that.

Britney   So you urny into him?

Celine   I didny say that either.

Whitney *appears and thumbs up* **Britney** *and waves her out.*
Britney *puts her hand out and* **Whitney** *gives her a wad of notes.*
Britney *goes towards the exit, triumphantly.*

Britney   Oh, and you should totally get oot ay they shite claes. Ronan'll realise you're a dug!

Britney *goes out.*

Celine   C'mere and say that, ya/

Celine *goes to follow* **Britney**.

Whitney   You've no let her get you on a downer?

Celine   I'm no on a downer, Whitney. I'm raging! She said Ronan only likes me because I'm pot ugly and I'll totally build his confidence up. And yet I've to help her get off with Ronan! I've changed my mind. I am on a downer! But it's no because ay her.

Whitney   What is it because ay?

Celine   Jarvis has gone off me!

Whitney   How do you work that out?

Celine   Mean, usually when me and him see each another we're like that. Only that last time there we wurny like that. We were more like that. He's feeding his face every five minutes. Prefers auld leftovers to me now!

Whitney   He is like that, isn't he? But so are you now, Celine.

Celine   I'm are not! I love my Jarvis so much it's!/ Or is he more like old bra and panties? Dead comfy, dead, dead boring?

Whitney   Well Jarvis is totally into – what is it? – localisation or something. Whereas you're more into being gorgeous an' gettin' guys tae like ye!

Celine   Are you saying I've no principles?

Whitney   No, I'm are not. Total honesty's one ay your principles.

Celine   So it is! But is one principle enough?

Whitney   Honesty's no your only one. Getting guys to like you's a principle tae!

Celine   Huvny heard ay that one! Is there a better way ay putting it?

Whitney   Aye, there is. It's the continuation of the species principle!

Celine   Oh, that is one ay ma principles!

Whitney   So when it comes to principles you could definitely aim your sights higher than Jarvis!

Celine   But nobody's got more principles than my Jarvis!

Whitney   Aye, OK, some guys has got less principles than Jarvis, but the less principles you've got the more likely you are to stick with them.

Celine   I totally know what you're talking about about him. He's all non-violent principles one minute, beating guys up the next. It's all conservation and saving the planet one day, then stuffing his greedy fat face while a billion poor wee Pakis are starving in the jungle the next. Then again, Whitney, I mind of I totally used to be like that: 'He's dead cute that Jarvis one, I totally wouldny mind continuing the species with him!'

Whitney   Thinking about dumping him then, Celine?

Celine   Och, don't ask me to think about dumping him! If I start thinking about it, I might start thinking about it. So I'm no gonny start thinking about it. But I canny help thinking about it now I've started thinking about it. And it's not as if I ever thought about it before I came to this place. So I'll have to get out ay here. But I canny. Because I huvny said cheerio to Brad yet. And I huvny said hello to Ronan yet. And I huvny got one o'er that wee bitch Britney yet.

And now I totally canny stop thinking about continuing the species wi' Brad. Or maybe even that creep Ronan. Which isny right. Because I shouldny want to continue the species wi' anyone except my Jarvis!

Whitney   Well, wi' the principle ay continuing the species you're supposed tae haud oan an' take the best offer you can get.

Celine   An' what about Jarvis?

Whitney   What about Jarvis?

Celine   I canny start dumping him. Can I?

Whitney   Aw, dumping people's part of the principle of continuing the species tae! The more the better! An' I thought you said he's gone off you?

Celine   So I did. So maybe I could get him to dump me. Because that would be a fuckofa lot easier than *me* dumping *him*! But how am I gonny get him to dump me? Mean, it's no even as if he's got off wi anyone else yet. An' who else is gonny want to get off wi' him?

Whitney   I know somebody!

Celine   Who, Whitney?

Whitney   Me, Celine.

Celine   . . . But Jarvis is a big fat boring cunt wi' a wee knob!

Whitney   That's the kinna guy I like. In fact, Celine (*Confidentially*.): that's the kinna guy I want to continue the species with! You angry with me?

Celine   Am I fuck. I'm chuffed with you. An' you're ma pal, aren't you? It isny as though you're one ay they wee bitches that would get satisfaction oot ay taking my boyfriend aff me. Is it, Whitney?

Whitney   Course no, Celine.

Celine   An' you know what, even if I wasny dumping Jarvis an' getting off wi' Brad or Ronan, I'd totally share the big fat cunt out wi' ye. As long as you take the wee knob.

Whitney   A wee knob suits me fine, Celine.

Celine   How come?

Whitney   Because *I've* got a wee fanny.

Ronan *appears, unseen to* **Celine**. **Whitney** *waves him to wait.*

Whitney   So a' you've to do now is make up your mind about whether it's Brad or Ronan!

Celine   But I don't even know anything about them. Not so much as a single solitary principle!

Whitney   Well, here's Brad now for you to ask him. I'll gie yeez five minutes.

Celine   Aw, thanks . . . Oh, an Whitney? . . . Brad asks me the size of my fanny, what'll I do? I mean: where'll I look?

Whitney   Straight at his knob! . . . Always your best bet. An' that way you'll find out if he's wanting to continue the species wi' you or not!

Whitney *goes up to the office. She opens window slightly so she can hear. She picks up cards and a marker.*

Ronan   You look like a princess!

Celine   Thought you'd of preferred me in they other claes!

Ronan   No way. These make you look uh, uh/

Whitney *holds up card with 'Principled' on it.* **Ronan** *sees it.*

Ronan   Well, I guess they make you look, uh, principled!

Celine   Do you like slags wi' principles?

Ronan   Sure do, ma'am. What ones you got?

Celine   Well, I'm committed to the honesty principle.

Ronan   Me too!

Celine   And the continuation of the species principle.

Ronan   That's one of mine. Any others?

Celine   Well/ Well, eh/ I believe in the loving people so much it's freaky principle. Heard ay it?

Ronan   I wrote that one!

Celine   That's amazing. You've got a' the same principles as me. Who would you tell you loved but?

Ronan   I ah/ I ah/

Whitney *holds up a card with 'Celine' on it.* **Ronan** *sees it.*

Ronan   I ah/ I ah/

Celine   Och, gonny no start stuttering!

Ronan   Well, I guess I'd tell my baby son I loved him.

Celine (*deflated*)   That's nice!

Ronan   Yip. I'd tell him every day.

Celine   Great.

Ronan   So he totally knew, you know?

Celine   Lovely. Anyone else?

Whitney *waves her 'Celine' card.* **Ronan** *sees it.*

Ronan   I ah/ I ah/ Who would you tell you loved?

Celine   Well, there's ma wee ma. I'd tell her. Then there's/ There's/

Ronan   Who, Celine?

Celine   Well, I/ well, I/ well, Jarvis, of course.

Ronan   No one else?

Celine   Naw! Well, aye. But I don't know if he/ if he/ I don't know if he loves me back. And he totally wouldny tell me if he did anyway. Because he's going back to America to run a coffee shop and I'll never see him again so I'll just have to totally slash my wrists and put an end to it a'.

Ronan Wowee!

Celine OK, I'm sorry. I shouldny've telt ye. It wisny fair ay me. An' now you'll probably hate my guts an' never/ Well, you'll never/ Well, will ye?

Whitney *puts up a sign with 'I love you' on it.* **Ronan** *sees it.*

Ronan I ah/ I ah/

Celine Och, I know. You just don't see *me* like I see *you*. But could you no just be Ronan instead ay that creep Ronan?

Whitney *puts a sign up: 'I'm Ronan'.* **Ronan** *sees it.*

Ronan I ah/ I ah/

Celine Could you no? An' what are you looking round at all the time?

Ronan I ah/ I ah/

Whitney *hides the sign and waves at* **Celine**. **Celine** *waves back.* **Whitney** *goes away from the window.*

Celine Great, isn't she, that Whitney? We've become total pals. Tell each another everything. No a bad bone in her body! An' how come if you're fae Yankeeland you stutter in Scottish?

Ronan I ah/ I ah/ I do?

Celine Och, it's all right. I'm no accusing you ay pittin it oan or anything.

Whitney *shows the 'I'm Ronan' card.* **Ronan** *sees it.*

Ronan I ah/ I ah/

Celine Because talkin' Scottish an' stutterin's more or less the same thing! I mean: what are you trying to tell me?

Whitney *waves her card.*

Ronan   I ah/ I ah/ Well, it's about Ronan.

Celine   Oh! What is it?

Ronan   He wants to meet you uptown tonight at the Shag Shack Club!

Celine   Well, I don't mind meetin' him. Are you takin' me?

Ronan   Sure thing!

Celine   Aw, thanks, Brad. An' I'll take ye to meet ma ma.

Ronan   Right now?

Celine   Aye! If we wait fer Jarvis tae come back he'll only go an' bring one ay his principles out and try an' stop me. 'Mon!

They go to go.

Ronan   What about Whitney?

Whitney *puts up a sign saying 'Go With Her!'* **Ronan** *sees it, forgets himself and nods at* **Whitney**. **Celine** *sees him nodding. She looks round.* **Whitney** *hides the card and waves.* **Celine** *waves back.*

Celine   Whitney's lovely. She willny mind. But come quick, before she comes down and starts training you. Because she can be a right bossy cow her!

Celine *takes* **Ronan** *by the hand and they rush out.* **Whitney** *looks quietly pleased and comes downstairs holding a card. She holds it up to the audience. It says: 'She'll regret calling me a cow!' Then she strolls out.*

Act Three

Next morning.
Whitney *is working upstairs in the office.* **Celine** *and* **Ronan** *come on together.* **Celine** *is in the clubbing clothes she changed into the day before.* **Ronan** *is carrying unmarked paper carrier bags. When* **Whitney** *realises they are there, she starts to pay attention.*

Celine   So this Ronan's turnt oot a total wank, Brad! Mean, a' the way tae the Shag Shack Club tae meet him an' he doesny even turn up!

Ronan (*Scottish*)   He'll've been held up.

Celine   I'll held up him when I meet him!

Pause.

But great night, wis it no?

Ronan   Brilliant!

Celine   An' you were dead, dead nice an' everything!

Ronan (*as if surprised*)   Wis I?

Celine   Slept in the exact same single bed at ma ma's when we stotted in frae the Shag Shack Club at a' oors an' ye didny even shag me!

Ronan   Did I no?

Celine   Well, we were pished out wur skulls, so you couldny've, could ye?

Ronan   Right enough!

Celine   Mean, ye totally know you've tae gie a slag respect an' no take advantage ay her. Don't you? . . . Well, don't you?

Ronan   Eh, well, actually, Celine doll:/

Celine   Celine doll what?

Ronan   I did so take advantage ay ye!

Celine (*as if surprised*)   Ye didny?

Ronan   Wid an apology dae?

Celine   Get tae fuck. I canny accept an apology fer that!

Ronan   Aw, how no?

Celine   No way! Because I know fine well you took advantage ay me! Thank fuck for which, by the way! Because you've got some size ay knob on ye! An' because ye totally gie'd me mare satisfaction than I've ever had in my whole entire puff! An' then when I had my climax wi' you shouting out a' yer principles an' that you were totally freaked out wi' love fur me, you totally took me to the next level! Did you reach it an' a'?

Ronan   Aye. An' it wis a stotter!

Celine   Aye, but was my pussy big enough for you?

Ronan   Ye've goat a smashin' big outsize pussy oan ye!

Celine   Aw, ye say the nicest things. Because it would need tae be outsize tae fit your outsized knob. But there's somethin' different about you the day. Canny think what it is! Can you?

Ronan   Naw! I canny.

Celine   Oha. You're totally talkin' in Scottish! Ya cheeky cunt ye. Scotland's only a poor wee place. Ye canny start rippin' the pish oot ay it.

Ronan   I widny dae that tae Scotland, Celine. Because when it comes to knobbin' an' shaggin' an' shootin' yer load, good auld Scottish's got tae be the best wee language in the whole entire world.

Celine   As long as it's good fer somethin', Brad, eh? An' this weekend might have started off shite but it's turned out a excellent one. But it willny last likely.

Ronan   Oh no?

Celine   No! Because Jarvis will be totally devastated when I tell him I shagged you.

Ronan   Maybe he won't be.

Celine   Don't say that. If Jarvis isny devastated, I'll be devastated. Because what's the point in spendin' hauf yer life with someone an' then dumpin' them if they urny gonny at least be devastated aboot it?

Ronan   Do you have to tell him?

Celine   Course I dae! Honesty's one ay ma principles! So I'm totally gonny find him an' tell him an' see if he's devastated. And mind an' no go back to Yankeeland an' no say goodbye!

Celine *goes out and* **Whitney** *comes down.*

Whitney   So ye spent the night wi' Celine, shagged her senseless, telt her ye love her but ye still didny tell her who ye are!

Ronan   She doesny like liars!

Whitney   No get very faur in the world wi'oot telling porkies!

Ronan   Celine and me're no wantin' tae get oan in the world!

Whitney   Aw, you're no back talking shite, are ye? Did yer night in a single bed in a damp coonsil hoose in Cunthill wi' a cheap slag no sort ye oot about a' that/?

Ronan   Naw, she isny a cheap slag! Well, she's no! An' a' ma night in a damp coonsil hoose in Cunthill done wis tae totally make me realise Celine an' Jarvis has got a' the right principles an' you an' ma da's got a' the wrang anes! Youse're screwing your workers and youse're screwing the third world an' globalisation has got to be stoaped before the whole entire planet's in the hauns ay hauf a dozen multinationals!

Whitney   Oh, Ronan!

Ronan   National governments a' sitting in the multinationals' pockets!

Whitney   Oh, Ronan, son.

Ronan   Voters the world o'er voting to get theirsels shagged up the arse! Can you no take me being committed tae a cause for the first time in ma life?

Whitney   It's no that, Ronan!

Ronan   So what is it? Mean, ma old man's been askin' me to pure commit masel', so he has. So noo I'm daein' it, is it gonny be a problem efter a'?

Whitney   It's no the commitment that's ca'd the feet fae under me.

Ronan   What is it well?

Whitney   It's you talking in Scottish wi'oot stuttering! How did ye manage it?

Ronan   Because/ Because Yankee's a shite language fer principles! Nae cunt wid believe ye!

Whitney   So when are ye gonny tell your da aboot yer new principles?

Ronan   Soon as the auld cunt gets back fae the Smoke! Is it no a good idea?

Whitney   It's a smashing idea! Your auld man'll love it. (*Aside.*) Will he fuck. But it puts me in direct line to the throne. And ye know what I'm like. Aye wantet to be Queen Whitney. Or no. Queen Whitney's tacky. But 'Business Wumman Ay The Year' would dae! Maybe wear a wee tiara at the award ceremony! (*To* **Ronan**.) An' what's that in your bag, Ronan? You been shopping? Gie your pal Whitney a swatch.

Ronan *opens his bag.* **Whitney** *takes a look and looks impressed.*

Whitney   Oh my fuck, Ronan. Go an' try them uh? Gie us all a treat!

Ringo *comes in as* **Ronan** *goes out with the bags.*

Ringo   Did Celine get back yet, Whitney? Jarvis's goin' aff his heid looking fur her! An' I wouldny mind, but it's ma day aff. An' I hardly got any sleep last night an'/

Whitney   Och, he is not.

Ringo   Going spare. Gonny kill her an' Ronan baith as soon as he stops stuffing his face wi' breakfast!

Whitney   Efter me spending the whole ay last night riding him tae kingdom come! The ungrateful swine!

Ringo   Did ye?

Whitney   Didny hurt your feelings, did I?

Ringo   Course no. Gie'd somebody a right good shagging masel' last night.

Whitney   Who was the lucky girl?

Ringo   Doesny matter!

Whitney   Och, you know ye can tell Whitney.

Ringo   Don't want tae embarrass her!

Whitney   Well, if ye see Jarvis, offer him a branch ay Costly Coffee to manage, gonny?

Ringo   Will that no be against his principles?

Whitney   His principles are beginning tae shoogle.

Ringo   Could ye no get someone else tae dae it? Piece ay nonsense this oan ma day aff. Guy wants tae pit his feet up oan his day aff. This place is getting ridiculous. Aye, oan at ye tae work yur day aff. Oan an' oan at ye. Oan an' oan an'/

Whitney   Who else can I ask?

Ringo   Ask my boy. Up in ma room, so he is. I'll get 'im fur ye. Tell him ye'll gie him a tenner. Dae anything for a tenner, so he will!

Whitney   Cheap, isn't he?

Ringo   What are you saying about ma boy, Whitney? My boy isny cheap. Competively priced, mibbe, I'll gie ye that.

Ringo *goes out.* **Whitney** *is about to go upstairs but she is stopped by* **Jarvis** *coming in, still eating a burger and carrying a can of juice, wearing fashion clothes.*

Jarvis   Where's my claes?

Whitney   I don't know. What's wrang wi' the ones you've got on?

Jarvis   What's right wi' them?

Whitney   So you don't like ma present?

Jarvis   Are they a present fae you?

Whitney   I thought you'd look hunky in them. An' ye know what, Jarvis: you dae. Do ye no like looking hunky?

Jarvis   Aye. I dae like lookin' hunky. But I shouldny.

Whitney   How no?

Jarvis   Because it's against ma principles tae look hunky! Have you seen Celine?

Whitney   Ye shouldny be asking about Celine.

Jarvis   How no?

Whitney   Because I spent the whole ay last night riding you to kingdom come's how no, Jarvis. So did you no enjoy it or what?

Jarvis   I totally loved it.

Whitney   Aw, you're just saying that!

Jarvis   I am not just saying it! Course I'm urny. You've got the best tight wee fanny I've ever shagged in my whole entire puff!

Whitney (*aside, moved*)   That's the nicest thing anyone ever said to me! (*To* **Jarvis**, *tough*.) So what are you going to dae aboot it?

Jarvis   What dae ye *want* me tae dae aboot it?

Whitney   For a start, you could show a bit ay gratitude an' tell me you love me so much it's freaky!

Jarvis   I was intending to tell you that!

Whitney   Well, shut up and tell me!

Jarvis   I canny. I've got tae dump Celine first!

Whitney   You mean you huvny dumped her yet?

Jarvis   I huvny seen her tae get dumping her, have I?

Whitney   Well, I'm heading till you dump her.

Whitney *goes to go*.

Jarvis   Nae ye urny!

Whitney   How no?

Jarvis   Because I'm no letting ye!

Jarvis *blocks her way*.

Whitney   Don't you dare get violent with me!

Jarvis   I'm urny getting violent.

Whitney   Aw, well, you might at least get violent!

Jarvis   All right, I'll get violent!

Whitney   Don't you dare get violent!

Jarvis   How no now?

Whitney   Because I might get to like it!

Jarvis   What's wrong with liking it?

Whitney   I'm no supposed to like it.

Jarvis   How are you no supposed to like it?

Whitney   Because I'm no going out with you!

Jarvis   You could be!

Whitney   No I couldny. You're going out with Celine!

Jarvis   No I'm no!

Whitney   Aye you are! You huvny dumped her!

Jarvis   Aye, but I will dump her.

Whitney (*aside*)   This conversation's doin' ma nut in. (*To* **Jarvis**.) Aye, but will ye?

Jarvis   Aye, I will. Naw, I willny. Well, I canny. Well, monogamy's one ay ma principles. An' I just don't want tae see that look ay disappointment a' o'er Celine's face when she finds oot her Jarvis has broken it!

Whitney   You've only tae tell her your principles has *changed*.

Jarvis   Your principles areny supposed tae change. That's the whole point ay having them.

Whitney   So you're no telling me you're still intae a' that anti-globalisation racket?

Jarvis   Aye, I'm are. Course I um. What of it?

Whitney   You're a lying slobby wee-knobbed hypocrite is what of it! You've got that many principles you canny tell your erse fae yer elbow is what of it! They a' contradict one another's what of it!

Jarvis *bursts into tears.*

Whitney   What are you greeting for?

Jarvis   You're . . . shouting . . . at . . . me!

Whitney   Well, you deserve tae be shouted at, wi' a' your shite!

Jarvis   I know, I know. So could you not help me?

Whitney   Help you how?

Jarvis   Tell me which principles to have and which to gie up!

Whitney   Gie them a' up! They're a' shite! Aye, gie them up an' get yersel' a better set!

Jarvis   Like what?

Whitney   A set that suits ye! Get yersel ones that'll allow ye to eat what ye want, wear what ye want, shag who ye want an' kick fuck oot ay who ye want!

Jarvis   Are there any like that?

Whitney   Hunners ay them. Get yersel some internationalist ones. Get some freedom ay aw the global mairkets ones. Get yoursel some embrace the *Zeitgeist* ones.

Jarvis   But the multinationals will end up running the show.

Whitney   When the multinationals are running the show, ye get the prices ay goods doon an' the variety up.

Jarvis   But wages go doon an' power gets concentrated in a few hands. Everyone else gets screwed.

Whitney   Get yersel some survival ay the fittest anes well! That way you get a' the excitement ay clawing yer way up till it's you that's ane ay the sets ay hauns you were talking aboot! An' look at it as natural!

Jarvis   Is there nobody you wouldny screw? What about your ain faimly?

Whitney   That's cried the continuation ay the species principle. Shag the best totty goin', get yer weans a wee bit love, their denner oan the table, then kick them tae fuck out, the using bamsticks! An' shag them up the erse if ye get any snash oot ay them while you're at it.

Jarvis   Aye, but I'm scared people think I'm a selfish cunt.

Whitney   You are a selfish cunt.

Jarvis   Aye, but should I no be trying to fight my ain nature an' totally rise above the bastard?

Whitney   Who dae ye think ye are trying to rise above yer ain nature?

If God had wantet you no tae be a selfish cunt he wouldny of made ye one in the first place!

Jarvis   It's no gonny be easy.

Whitney   Course it isny. A's you've tae dae is stert liking yersel, selfish cunt an' a'.

Jarvis   Will you help me?

Whitney   Aye, I'll help you. Oan one condition.

Jarvis   What's that?

Whitney (*suddenly girly*)   That you tell me you love me so much it's freaky!

Jarvis   I dae love you so much it's freaky! Is that no obvious? Mean: it's takin me a' my life tae find a tight wee fanny like yours an' someone tae tell me which principles tae huv, I'm no giein' ye up noo!

Whitney   Do you mean it but?

Jarvis   I totally one hundred per cent mean it, Whitney.

Whitney (*aside*)   Oh my fuck, he means it. What am I gonny dae when Marlon gets back? (*To* **Jarvis**.) You're a wee smasher, so you are. Dead, dead masterful and dominant!

Jarvis (*flattered*)   Am I?

Whitney   Definitely!

Damon *appears.* **Whitney** *signals him to wait.*

Whitney   So are you ready tae tell Celine she's dumped?

Jarvis   I think so.

Whitney   Are you or aren't you?

Jarvis   Which principle do I use?

Whitney   The continuation ay the species principle, prick. A's yurr daein's in takin' me's taking the best totty that's on offer.

Jarvis   Thanks.

Whitney   Will you manage it now?

Jarvis   Course. I'll blow Celine away, so I will. I've hated the ugly cow ever since I met her. Wi' her outsize fanny an' her no havin' any ay her ain principles an' wantin me tae gie her ma ones!

Whitney (*aside*)   This guy is getting more hunkier by the second! (*To* **Jarvis**.) I'll go and get her for ye!

Jarvis   I'll come with you.

Whitney   You're all right!

Jarvis   I'm coming!

Whitney   If you love me you'll do as I say!

Jarvis   What principle is that based on?

Whitney   The knowing when you're beat principle!

Jarvis   You are such a ride, Whitney!

Whitney (*aside*)   He means it!

Jarvis   Aw, Whitney!

Whitney   What?

Jarvis   Noo I'm an assimilated capitalist cunt, what the fuck am I gonny dae wi' the rest ay ma life?

Whitney You're just aboot tae funn oot.

Jarvis What?

As **Whitney** *goes out, she waves* **Damon** *in.*

Jarvis (*aside*) Fuck me slowly!

Damon Met Ronan, so I did. An he's dead chuffed wi' ye.

Jarvis What fer?

Damon Because you got a big fat cunt wi' a wee knob tae get off wi' Whitney.

Jarvis What of it?

Damon He's like that: Tell the big fat cunt I'll gie him a Costly Coffee shop to manage's what of it, my man!

Jarvis What dae I want a Costly Coffee shop tae manage fur?

Damon Pure buzz managing a Costly Coffee shop. Pure buzz, my man. Guys would pure look up to you. Own Costly Coffee shop tae manage! Know what I mean?

Jarvis I don't want guys looking up at me.

Damon How no, man? How no?

Jarvis Because I'd end up liking them looking up at me and get assimilated! (*Aside.*) What the fuck am I talking about? I am assimilated!

Damon It's a pure buzz, man: guys looking up at you!

Jarvis Do guys look up at you?

Damon No, man. No. Be a pure buzz though, man. A pure buzz.

Jarvis OK, a buzz guys looking up at me. Be a pure buzz. But I don't want guys looking up at us for managing a Costly Coffee shop, dae I?

Damon   How no but, my man? How no?

Jarvis   Because I want guys tae look up at me fur going round sticking up for my principles! I want guys tae look up at us for defending the right ay Costly Coffee tae make every coffee served the globe o'er a Costly one! I want guys tae look up at us for getting a' the creepy government guys tae sit in Costly Coffee's pocket an' dae exactly what Costly Coffee tells them tae dae. I want guys tae look up at us for making Costly Coffee embrace the *Zeitgeist*! You willny get that managing a Costly Coffee shop. A' you'll get managing a Costly Coffee shop's creeps like you moanin' an' groanin' behind your back about their shite working conditions an' wantin' mare pay when the backslidin' twats don't deserve it!

Damon   So take a Costly Coffee tae manage, uh? Should, my man. Totally should!

Jarvis   For the last time, I don't want ane!

Damon   How no, man? How no?

Jarvis   Because it's no a Costly Coffee shop I'll be managing. It's a Costly Coffee *area*.

Damon   Aw, Ronan'll gie ye an area!

Jarvis   I don't want an area, I want a country!

Damon   Ronan'll totally gie ye a country! You've only tae say the word!

Jarvis   I don't want a country either, prick!

Damon   What dae ye want?

Jarvis   I want the *whale* ay Costly Coffee tae manage!

Damon   Likely gie ye the whale ay Costly Coffee, so he will. Good guy, Ronan. Excellent.

Jarvis   Right, you can head now!

Damon   I'm heading, man. I'm heading.

Jarvis   Well, head well! And I hope yer faimly shags ye up the arse.

Damon   My faimly does shag me up the arse! Ma auld man shagged me up the arse last night, so he did!

Jarvis   Ya dirty poof, ye!

Damon   Aw, that isny oan, neither it is.

Jarvis   What isny?

Damon   Talking aboot oppressed minorities like that!

Jarvis   Aye, there'll be zero tolerance ay oppressed minorities when I'm runnin' Costly Coffee. Now head!

Damon   And I don't do actual poofery, by the way.

Jarvis   What dae ye dae?

Damon   Business, my man. I do business. The same as you. An' it's well paid an' a'.

Jarvis   How much dae ye get?

Damon   Tenner, man. Auld man, Ringo gie'd me a tenner last night, so he did! Gie hauf it tae me auld ma, so I will.

Jarvis   A tenner's fuck a'! You're needing tae get your ideas sorted oot an' quadruple yer earnings!

Damon   How am I gonny dae that?

Jarvis   Get your arsehole advertised, man. Gie your arsehole an international outlook. In fact: get your arsehole branded!

Damon   Branded wi' what?

Jarvis   Eh, eh, High Quality Arsehole? No. Too boring. And it'll need to be plural. Ye need guys tae think yeez are a big global outfit wi' mare than ane wee arsehole sitting in ane wee room somewhere. So how about, eh, Assertive

Arseholes? No. Put timid wee nervous knobs like mine aff
that would. I eh/ I eh/ I've got it!

Damon   What, my man? What?

Jarvis   *Aromatic* Arseholes!

Damon   Aw thanks, my man. Sounds great, my man.
(*Chanting with increasing confidence as he exits.*) Aromatic
Arseholes! Aromatic Arseholes! Aromatic Arseholes!

Damon *is so absorbed with his new idea, he doesn't notice* **Ringo**
coming in.

Ringo   Fuck's up wi' ma boy!

Jarvis   You takin' advantage ay him's what's up wi' him!

Ringo   Naw I huvny!

Jarvis   You trying tae say you didny shag him up the arse
last night?

Ringo   Course I didny. Well, I did. But I didny have
anyone else tae shag, did I? Wi' you shagging Whitney an'
no sharin' her oot. An' it doesny make me a poof, by the
way.

Jarvis   How dae ye work that out?

Ringo   Because I was thinking ay Whitney while I was
shagging him! An' there's nothing wrang wi' shagging yer
boy! He's faimly! An' faimly's fuck a' use tae ye except tae
shag! Mean, how else are ye supposed tae learn how tae get
shagged if it's no by yer faimly, ya tube?

Jarvis   It was against ma auld principles no tae shag my
faimly, no ma new anes! An' it isny teaching yer boy tae be
a poof ye should be ashamed ay!

Ringo   What is it well?

Jarvis   No teaching yer boy a proper foundation in
capitalism an' how tae get a hauf-decent price fur his arse!

Ringo   Aye, but he's no got much ay an arse. Mean, if it was Whitney's arse we were talking aboot I'd maybe slip her an extra fiver! An' if ye see her tell her the big man's back.

Jarvis   Who's the big man?

Ringo   Marlon O'Donnell! The owner ay Costly Coffee.

Jarvis   Aw ace, man. Get tae meet him at long last. Now get oot, staff!

Ringo   You canny talk tae me like that! This is ma day aff! I'm no having it! I should be back in ma room giein' my boy another shaggin, so I should. Usually gies me two fur the price ay ane, the boy.

Jarvis   Aye, nae mare!

Ringo   What?

Jarvis   Yur boy's arsehole's gone global!

Ringo   Aw, ye huvny shoved a globe up ma boy's arse? That's ridiculous. You'll have it a' stretched tae buggery! I'll need tae get his arsehole took fer treatment! An' what if his arsehole doesny recover! That wee arsehole's ma boy's livelihood! I'm away. I'll need tae see if I can get a discount off ma boy fer no gettin' ma second shag! Mean, what's the world coming tae? (**Ringo** *goes to exit, shaking his head as he chants.*) Ane shag fer a tenner! Ane shag fer a tenner! Ane shag fer a tenner!

Ringo *exits, oblivious to* **Ronan**'s *entrance.* **Ronan** *is now wearing ecowarrier clothes.*

Jarvis (*aside*)   Who's this now? An' look at the state ay im. Ye get shot ay ane wank, an' anither ane turns up! An' I totally don't recognise him. Which is well weird. I know every ecowarrier this side ay Suckingcock Street. This cunt isny ane ay them! (*To* **Ronan**.) Don't expect tae see guys like you round here!

Ronan   No?

Jarvis   Well, when it comes tae globalised capitalism, it's a bit ay a hotspot, you know?

Ronan   No for much longer, I hope.

Jarvis   Aw, time you packed a' that shite in, Jim, an' totally acted your age an' changed your principles! An' I don't recognize ye. Were ye at the protest?

Ronan   What protest?

Jarvis   So what are ye daein' here? An' what bam let ye in in that state?

Ronan   I live here.

Jarvis   Naw! (*Confidentially.*) Are ye like fighting globalized capitalism fae the inside? If so, you should get a' that shite aff. Ye need tae learn tae *disguise* yer principles!

Ronan   What would I want tae disguise my principles fur? I've only just found them.

Jarvis   But that creepy wee cunt Ronan will chuck ye oot when he sees ye!

Ronan   Naw he willny!

Jarvis   How do you work that out?

Ronan   Because I'm Ronan!

Jarvis   Naw ye urny!

Ronan   Aye I am!

Jarvis   Well, what the fuck are ye Ronan fur?

Ronan   I canny exactly help it.

Jarvis   Did you shag ma Celine?

Ronan   Aye I did. What of it?

Jarvis   Well c'mere till I kick fuck oot ye!

Ronan   Ye urny gonny get violent are ye?

Jarvis   Course no. It's against ma principles tae get violent! So fer accusing me of gonny get violent an' shaggin' ma Celine before I dumped her I'm gonny get violent! But I'm no gonny get violent.

Ronan   How no?

Jarvis   Because you're the best thing that ever happened tae me!

Ronan   You're the best thing that ever happened tae me!

Jarvis   If it hadny of been fer you accosting ma Celine I wouldny have come here and changed a' my principles!

Ronan   An' if it hadny of been fer you giein' a' yer principles tae Celine, she wouldny of gie'd me them! So dae ye know what, big man?

Jarvis   What, wee man?

Ronan   I love you so much it's freaky!

Jarvis   I love you so much it's freaky!

They embrace.

But yer principles are shite! Ha ha.

Ronan   An' yours suck, by the way! Ha ha. So could you dae me a favour an' tell that Celine slag she's dumped? End ay hassle!

Jarvis   Naw I canny, wee man!

Ronan   Aw, how no, big man?

Jarvis   That's ma Celine we're talking about. I canny dump ma Celine. Can you no get her tae dump me?

Ronan   It should be up tae you.

Jarvis   How dae ye work that out?

Ronan   You're the ane that changed your principles!

Jarvis   Quite right tae change ma principles, ya inward-looking anti-globalising fanny!

Ronan *goes to go.*

Jarvis   C'mere, you! I huvny finished telling ye what I think ay ye. Where are ye going?

Ronan   Tae tell Celine no tae bother dumping ye. She'll only have tae wipe ye aff her arse, ya hard-nosed capitalist gobshite!

Ronan *goes one way as* **Celine** *comes in another.*

Jarvis   Aye, c'mere an' say that ya/ Celine, doll!

Celine   What?

Jarvis   I eh/ I eh/ How was your night?

Celine   No bad. Yours?

Jarvis   Same!

Short pause.

Celine   Did ye miss me at a'?

Jarvis   Course I missed you. You miss me?

Celine   Course!

Short pause.

Jarvis   You no gonny say anything?

Celine   Are you no?

Jarvis   Well, I heard you'd something tae say tae me.

Celine   That's what I heard about you.

Jarvis   So did ye?

Celine   Sort ay, aye. Did you?

Jarvis   Same.

Short pause.

What is it?

Celine   Well, I heard ye wanted me tae dump you tae save you dumping me.

Jarvis   That's what I heard about you!

Celine   So dae ye want tae dump me?

Jarvis   What if I dae?

Celine   Ya cheeky cunt, ye. Ye urny dumping me!

Jarvis   Get tae fuck. I'll dump ye if I want.

Celine   I'm dumping you first!

Jarvis   I decided before you!

Celine   I decided before you!

Jarvis   So when did you decide?

Celine   While Brad was shagging me reciting his principles! You?

Jarvis   While Whitney was shagging me reciting hers!

Celine   I canny believe you shagged that ugly cow!

Jarvis   I canny believe you let that Yankee knobhead shag you!

Celine   See you sometime then, tosser.

Celine *goes to go.*

Jarvis   Aye, see you, slag!

Jarvis *goes to go another way.*

Celine   Where dae ye think you're gauin'?

Jarvis   Gettin' the fuck away fae you!

Celine   But it's me that's walking out an' leavin' you!

Jarvis   Tell you what: we'll no be petty. We'll leave at the exact same time! (*Sarcastic.*) An' good luck tae ye!

Celine (*sarcastic*)   Aye, an' good luck tae you!

They both go to go, now reluctantly.

Celine   Oh, an' Jarvis!

Jarvis   What, Celine, doll?

Celine   Great we could be dead, dead mature an' totally part on good terms, innit?

Jarvis   That's just what I was thinking, Celine! Cheers!

Celine   Cheers tae you too, Jarvis!

Jarvis *goes out one way and* **Celine** *goes to go out another only to run into* **Ronan** *coming in.*

Celine   I done it, Brad boy. An' I was like that: nae messin', straigh oot wi' it!

Ronan   How'd he take it?

Celine   Aw, pure roarin' an' greetin' an' beggin' me tae stay on wi' him.

Ronan   Did he?

Celine   Did he fuck. O, he wanted tae. But ye know what these capitalists are like: canny show their feelin's in case ye get one o'er them! But the good thing wis we totally parted oan good terms!

Ronan   You did not?

Celine   Course we didny. I just pure let him *think* we did. Well, you canny show these capitalists yer bitter an' twisted feelin's an' let *them* get ane o'er *you*. So we'll just get up the road hame tae ma ma's an' have ane last shag before you fuck aff back to Yankeeland! 'Mon!

They go to go

Celine   Shame I never got tae meet Ronan but! Pure wouldny of minded gobbing in the creepy cunt's face!

Ronan   You have met him.

Celine   Och, I have not. Where was this?

Ronan   Here.

Celine   When?

Ronan   The now!

Celine   You mean he's coming?

Ronan   He's here already!

Celine   Where the fuck is he then?

Ronan   Standing right beside you!

Celine   No he isny. No he's no. No he's/ Oh fuck! Oh my sweet fanny! Oh my/

Ronan   Sorry about that!

Celine   What are you sorry for?

Ronan   Fer no tellin' ye sooner.

Celine   Well, you shouldny be sorry. It gie'd me a chance tae get tae know ye before I knew it wis you I was gettin' tae know! But how come you *didn't* tell me who you are?

Ronan   Well, I wanted ye tae want me for me and no fer my/ my/

Celine   But you huvny goat any/ any/ Oh my fuck, you do have money! You're the heir ay/ But what are ye gonny dae wi' it?

Ronan   Fuck knows!

Celine   You're no keepin' it, are ye? You canny. A' that money's against yer principles. Ye'll need tae gie it tae the Ecowarriers ay Cunthill! Fancy it?

Ronan   I eh/ I eh/

Marlon (*off*)   Anyone in there?

Celine   Who's that?

Ronan It's my/ It's ah/ Ah/

Ronan *goes to go.*

Celine Where are you away to?

Ronan I ah/ I ah/ I gotta practise my/

Celine If ye're practisin' no stuttering I'll gie ye a hand!

Ronan *and* **Celine** *go out one way as* **Marlon** *comes in another.*

Marlon *pours himself coffee, takes a croissant and goes up the stairs. He should look unwell and could show this by taking a rest halfway up. As he goes into the office,* **Jarvis** *and* **Whitney** *come on.*

Marlon *sits to work at the computer but he notices he has been joined a little way into the scene. He turns and watches.*

Whitney Well, thank fuck fer that! How did she take it?

Jarvis Oh, roarin' an' greetin' an' callin' me a capitalist gobshite! Then she was gonny pure walk oot on us, man. So I just rose above it a', an' told her her fanny wisny a patch oan your ane an' left it at that! Because, see, these anti-capitalists, Whitney, you know what it is wi' them, don't ye?

Whitney What is it, Jarvis?

Jarvis Envy!

Marlon *comes out of the office and down the stairs very slowly.*

Jarvis So I wanted tae say something else tae ye.

Whitney What?

Jarvis I love you so much it's freaky!

Short pause.

Jarvis Are ye no happy noo, Whitney?

Whitney Naw, I'm no. Aye, I am. Well, I'm no.

Jarvis Ye wanted me tae say I loved ye before I dumped Celine, didn't ye?

Whitney   Aye, I did. But that isny why I'm unhappy.

Jarvis   Well, why are ye unhappy?

Whitney   Aw, yer no expecting me tae tell ye, are ye?

Jarvis   How am I no tae?

Whitney   Because ye'll dump me if I tell ye!

Jarvis   Nothing you tell me could make me dump ye!

Whitney   Well, I'm seeing someone else!

Jarvis   You what?

Whitney   See! I knew ye'd dump me! Which is a total scandal after you standin' there an' promising you wouldny. An' after me promising masel *I'd* dump *him*.

Jarvis   You're gonny?

Whitney   Aye, I'm gonny!

Jarvis   Well, that's all right then!

Whitney   Is it?

Jarvis   Course! I came wi' baggage tae, remember! Now can I rip yer knickers aff an'/

Whitney   Naw ye canny!

Jarvis   How no?

Whitney   Because it's offensive tae women!

Jarvis   Fuck women! Mean: at ane point my auld principles would of totally stopped me talking dirty in case it was offensive tae women. But a' that's behind me noo! An' who's this guy yer seein'?

They realise **Marlon** *is standing beside them.*

Whitney   Oh, hiya, Marlon!

Marlon *nods.*

Whitney   An' this is Jarvis!

Jarvis Aw, you're no Marlon O'Donnell, are ye?

Marlon *nods.*

Jarvis I've always wanted tae meet you. You're an icon ay mine! You're the first genuine global capitalist bastard I've met. Good on ye.

Jarvis *shakes* **Marlon**'s *hand vigorously.*

Whitney So did ye sign, Marlon?

Marlon *nods.*

Whitney Aw, ace man! Jarvis: Costly Coffee has took o'er the Coffee Company ay America!

Jarvis Wow!

Whitney But yer no yersel, Marlon. Want a wee seat?

Helped by **Jarvis**, *she sits him down.*

There you are, drink yer coffee! That'll revive you. But weren't ye supposed tae bring me back a wee surprise.

Marlon *nods.*

Whitney Well, what is it?

Marlon (*with massive effort*) I've . . . put . . . the . . . European . . . shops . . . out . . . to . . . franchise!

Whitney Aw, Marlon, ya beauty.

She hugs a bewildered **Marlon**.

That's magic ay ye. An'/ An'/

Ronan *and* **Celine** *come on.*

Whitney Yer da's ta'en no well, Ronan. This is Ronan's da, Celine.

Celine How's it gauin?

Whitney Tired after the trip, that's a'. (*To* **Ronan**.) Tell him yer news. Cheer yer da up!

Ronan   I ah/ I ah/

Whitney   Noo's yer chance, son. He's got a temporary loss ay his voice. He'll no able tae answer ye back. Ha ha.

Ronan   Well, I ah/ I ah/

Whitney *leaves* **Marlon**'s *side to help* **Ronan**.

Whitney   Breathe, Ronan. Mind and breathe.

Ronan's *speech fights for attention with* **Marlon** *getting up off his chair very slowly and fighting to speak. During it,* **Whitney** *prevents* **Jarvis** *from butting in.*

Ronan (*egged on physically by* **Celine**)   It's a' o'er between me and Costly Coffee, da . . . I've had enough ay you screwing yer workers, screwing the public and screwing the third world. An' I willny be ca'in' ye da any more, da. Fae noo oan, it's war! Fae noo oan I'm wi' the Ecowarriors ay Cunthill an you're wi the/

Ronan's *speech is finally fatally undermined by* **Marlon**'s *spectacular zigzagging walk which nearly comes to grief several times before he finally has a seizure and collapses. There is a long shocked pause before they all rush in.* **Whitney** *takes his pulse.*

Jarvis   Is he all right, Whitney?

Whitney   Naw he isny.

Jarvis   Whit's wrang wi' him?

Whitney   Whit's right wi' him? He's deid!

Jarvis   Are you sure, Whitney? Could ye no pump his tits?

Whitney   He's deid, Jarvis. He liked gettin' his tits pumped when he was alive. Wouldny be dignified noo. Imagine pumpin' the tits ay a corpse! What are ye like?

Jarvis *burst into tears.*

Whitney   Aw, whit's wrang wi' ye noo? It should be Ronan that's greetin', no you!

Jarvis   He wis the first capitalist icon I got tae meet an he's died oan me before we can get a hauf-decent exchange ay views!

Celine   You all right, Ronan?

Ronan   Och aye!

Celine   You sure? I mean, he might ay been a capitalist cunt but he wis yer da! Did ye no love him?

Ronan   Naw!

Celine   How no?

Ronan   He didny love me!

Celine   Bastard! A' the same they capitalists. Better aff deid!

Whitney   Aye, he did love ye, ya prick!

Celine   Well, he should of showed it well!

Whitney   No showin' it wis his way ay showing it!

Celine   Didny work, did it? Ronan's got the exact opposite principles fae him. Don't ye?

Ronan   Aye!

Celine   An' he's selling aff Costly Coffee an giein' a' the money tae Ecowarriors ay Cunthill.

Whitney   Wouldny dae that tae yer da, wid ye?

Ronan   No. Course I wouldny. Sorry, Celine!

Celine   But Ecowarriors ay Cunthill would be set up fer life! How no?

Ronan   Because it wid be against ma principles! I don't want tae begin ma new life wi' the Ecowarriors oan the wrong foot. We urny fightin' globalised capitalism wi' globalized capitalism's money. So I'm gonny walk away right now an' leave it tae them! Are ye coming?

Celine Try an' stoap me. You've got the best wee set ay principles this side ay Suckingcock Street.

Celine and **Ronan** go out, hand in hand.

Jarvis I canny believe this a' happened by chance, Whitney!

Whitney A' what?

Jarvis You an' me thegither an' the heids ay a global empire a' in twenty-four hours!

Whitney It didny happen by chance!

Jarvis How did it happen?

Whitney That's a fuckofa fuckofa fuckofa long story! Ye ready tae shag me yet?

Jarvis I telt ye, Whitney. I'll shag ye when ye get the other guy dumped.

Whitney Och, I don't need to dump him noo, dae I?

Jarvis Aye, ye dae! Because noo I'm the heid ay a global empire, I canny be walkin' into board meetin's an' they're a' sniggering behind their agendas because ma slag's shagging around. Can I?

Whitney But I canny dump him now, Jarvis.

Jarvis How no?

Britney comes in, laden with label bags.

Britney Heh, Whitney. C'mere till ye see what I got wi' that money ye gie'd me.

Whitney That's smashin', Britney. Ye got loads, didn't ye?

Britney No I did not, Whitney. I didny get half ay what I wanted! So gonny gie us mare seein' as how I helped ye get that big fat cunt offa Celine . . . An' who's this? Oh my fuck. It's him!

Jarvis   Have you been usin' me, Whitney?

Whitney   Aye, I used ye. Because I wisny expectin' tae fa' in love wi' ye, wis I? Dae ye mind?

Britney *sees* **Marlon**'s *body and goes over to it.*

Jarvis   Course I don't mind, Whitney!

Whitney   How no?

Jarvis   Because fair's fair: usin' each another's what good capitalists do! Aw, naw, as long as ye get him dumped, we've still got a future!

Britney   She willny have to dump Marlon!

Whitney   Shut up, Britney!

Britney   Look! He's deid! Have youse no noticed?

Whitney   Sorry!

Jarvis   What are ye sorry for? Imagine me pullin' the slag ay a global capitalist. Must of pure arrived now!

Britney *becomes absorbed in her shopping.*

Whitney   So everything's all right then?

Jarvis   Aye, it's all right. Course it is. As long as ye get him dumped!

Whitney   But he's deid, Jarvis. Ye canny dump a corpse!

Jarvis   Get him dumped, I said. An' I'll maybe shag ye after lunch.

Whitney *watches* **Jarvis** *go out and goes to* **Marlon**. *She strokes him gently and she becomes increasingly sexual with him before mounting him and motioning shagging him.* **Britney** *is still absorbed in her shopping.*

Whitney (*starting tenderly and becoming increasingly aggressive*) You're dumped, Marlon darlin'. You're dumped, Marlon darlin'. You're dumped! You're dumped! You're dumped!

Her chanting continues as the lights fade.